PEARSON
PUBLISHING

Student Handbook
for History

Bernard Barker, Elizabeth Robinson, Carl Smith
and Mel Vlaeminke

Cartoons by Steve Clarke

Illustrations by Julie Beer

Student Handbook for History

Name *Charlotte Green*

Class *U3K (Room 8)*

School *Bury Grammar School (Girls)*

Dates of tests or exams:

1 ....

2 ....

3 ....

Exam board ....

Syllabus numbers...

Candidate number..

Centre number ....

Further copies of this publication may be obtained from:

Pearson Publishing
Chesterton Mill, French's Road, Cambridge CB4 3NP
Tel 01223 350555   Fax 01223 356484

Email info@pearson.co.uk   Web site http://www.pearson.co.uk/education/

ISBN: 1 85749 581 0

Published by Pearson Publishing 1999
© Pearson Publishing 1999

Contents

Foreword

Historical skills play a major part in Key Stage 3 and GCSE History. Historical terminology can be confusing and you may worry about how to tackle source-based assignments, for example. This handbook is designed to help you by illustrating the five main historical skills (Key Elements) required by the National Curriculum, ie:

- 1 Chronology

- 2 Range and depth of historical knowledge and understanding

- 3 Interpretations of history

- 4 Historical enquiry

- 5 Organisation and communication.

Each chapter clarifies one of the key skills involved in historical study, explains how to approach tasks and provides sample answers. A practice question using sources is included in every chapter. Original sources are included and attributed. In addition, some sources have also been created to help illustrate particular points.

The handbook aims to demonstrate how you can achieve higher levels or grades. It can also aid your revision of the subject because the chapters cover all the major topics included in the National Curriculum and in GCSE syllabuses.

You can check your progress and understanding at both Key Stage 3 and GCSE against a checklist of the requirements for each grade or level. The contents page can be used as a checklist as you work through the book. A page for your own notes is included at page 120.

Introduction

The 1066 Rap

After Edward's last Confession in 1066,
England was left in quite a fix.
Harold took over but not for long;
Breaking a promise was what he'd done wrong.

The throne had been promised to several others,
Including a mate of Harold's brother.
Tostig and Hardrada invaded the North
And forced Harold's army to sally forth.

Then William, sailing from Normandy,
Landed down south near Pevensey.
Victory in the north but another long trek
Turned the Saxon army into a wreck.

In a landmark battle down Hastings way,
The Norman archers carried the day.
Harold died, the Conqueror won;
England's Middle Ages had begun.

This light-hearted poem is about a very important episode in English history. What does it tell us?

- it gives a version of the main events in 1066
- it mentions five main characters (Edward, Harold, Tostig, Hardrada and William)
- it mentions three places (Normandy, Pevensey and Hastings) and two regions (North and South)
- it gives a few clues about why things happened as they did.

But is it a good piece of history? What would make it better as a historical account? What would you need to do to produce a better historical account?

You would need more information about the five main characters, ie:

- which countries did they come from?
- which positions did they hold?
- do we know anything else about their backgrounds?

This could lead you to discover more about the countries or regions they came from, eg:

- where on a map of Western Europe are they?
- were they rich or poor, powerful or weak?
- who were the Saxons and the Normans?

These investigations are all to do with increasing your Historical knowledge (Key Element 2), so that you are better informed about the people involved, where they came from, etc.

William finally conquered his NRA

Then find out more about why the five men were all in England in 1066:

- what were the promises which seem to be the cause of the trouble?

- who had promised what to whom?

You are beginning to understand the causes, an important aspect of Historical understanding (also Key Element 2). Chapter 2 of this handbook helps you to develop your skills relating to Key Element 2.

Next try to construct a picture of what happened during 1066, thinking of the times and the places:

- for each of the verses of the poem, where were the main characters?

- so who was on the move?

- what was the sequence of events — in what order did things happen?

- can you find out how long the journeys and the battles took?

You could draw a map of England, marking on the important places, and who went where.

You could also construct a timeline of the events of 1066 — this is called Chronology (Key Element 1). Chapter 1 helps you to develop your skills in Chronology.

You have probably by now understood some of the more puzzling words in the poem:

- are you clear about the meaning of *sally forth* and *trek*?

Sally Forth to Captain Kirk...
Come in Kirk...

- are you clear about the meaning of *landmark* and *invasion*?

These show that you need to become familiar with certain words and terms which are commonly used in history, so that you too can use 'the vocabulary of history'. Other examples are *peasantry, treaty, reform* and *republic*. Sometimes words have a particular meaning in history which may be different from how they are used in other contexts. You may have looked up the meaning of some of the words in the poem and still not really understood them.

- why do the words *Confession* and *Conqueror* have capital letters?

This is because some words convey a quite complicated idea or concept. Although the circumstances will change from one historical event to another, the concept still means the same, eg empire, revolution, democracy. Being able to select and use the right term is a very important historical skill, which is part of Organisation and communication (Key Element 5). Chapter 5 of this handbook helps you to develop your skills relating to Key Element 5.

In this poem, the word *Confession* has a particular meaning, because King Edward became known as Edward the Confessor, to show he was a very religious man. So to understand this word fully, you would need to find out more about what confession is, what religion was strong at the time, etc.

You may need extra information to make the poem more historically accurate:

- where would you look for that extra information?

The more he looked into it, the bigger it became!

- are there some pictures or objects to help, or places to visit?
- would you know if the information you found was good?

These questions relate to the skills of Historical enquiry (Key Element 4), which requires you to investigate topics for yourself; to be able to collect and record a range of sources of information; and to use them in a fruitful way. Chapter 4 deals with this.

In other words, you have to become something of a detective — looking for clues and weighing up which are good ones and which are not.

Sometimes you can be really puzzled by different versions of an historical event which do not agree:

- is there any way you could find out more about the promises mentioned in this poem?
- if everyone seems to have been promised the English throne, what factors would influence you in deciding who was right?

This is the skill of Interpretations of history (Key Element 3). Chapter 3 deals with this. You do not have to accept someone else's view; you can weigh up the evidence for yourself and explain your own opinion.

For example, a popular version of the Norman Conquest (*Horrible Histories*) writes about the 'nasty Normans', 'Bloodthirsty Bill' and 'Billy the Bully'. Do you think a French person would have written that? How might 'Les Histoires Horribles' describe Harold and the Saxons?

William was hurt by being called a 'Nasty Norman'

Each of the chapters in this handbook:

- helps you develop historical skills and understanding
- enables you to link the key elements and skills of the National Curriculum to the main periods and topics taught at school
- explains the concepts and terminology used about each historical period you study
- helps you plan answers using appropriate historical skills
- shows you examples of good answers for each National Curriculum level
- guides you through the main features of each period
- provides a timeline
- enables you to test your skills and move to higher levels using evidence-based activities.

1 Chronology

This chapter introduces the main themes and concepts you need to understand to answer questions about life and society in the Middle Ages (1066-1500). As you study, you will apply information from a range of sources to place events, people and changes within a chronological framework and use dates, terms and conventions to describe past time.

Chronology (derived from the Greek word for time) is the method we use to put events in the order in which they happened. Historians place people, events and changes in time periods, to which they give names. The table below shows the different periods and names covered by the National Curriculum:

Out of order things sense just make didn't

Medieval Realms: 1066-1500

Historian's name	Royal name	Main event name	Political or social system name
Middle Ages	Norman, Plantagenet, etc	Norman Conquest	Feudalism

The Making of the United Kingdom: Crowns, Parliaments and Peoples 1500-1750

Early Modern	Tudor, Stuart	Reformation or Civil War	Monarchy

Britain 1750-c1900

Modern	Hanoverian, Victorian	Industrial Revolution	Imperialism

The Twentieth-Century World (after 1900)

Contemporary	Windsor	Total War	Democracy

Things that happen make better sense when they are placed in order and grouped together. The hour glass printed below measures passing time. Test your understanding by labelling each of the events in the boxes below, 1 to 5, to show where it fits in the flow of time. Don't worry about exact dates but get the events in the right order. Look up the events in a history textbook or an encyclopedia if you are not sure when they happened.

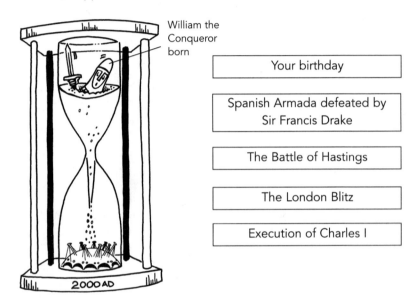

William the Conqueror born

| Your birthday |

| Spanish Armada defeated by Sir Francis Drake |

| The Battle of Hastings |

| The London Blitz |

| Execution of Charles I |

To apply a chronological framework effectively you:

- place events and objects in order of time *(Level 1)*
- describe changes over a period of time *(Level 2)*
- identify the similarities and differences between periods *(Level 3)*
- describe the characteristics of past societies and periods *(Level 4)*
- identify change and continuity within and across periods *(Level 5)*
- tell the difference between different kinds of historical change. *(Level 6)*

Level 3

To achieve Level 3, you must be aware that the past can be divided into different periods of time and recognise similarities and differences between these periods, using dates and terms appropriately. Complete this activity:

Activity

Tick box A or box B below to indicate the correct period for each fact:

Period A   Medieval realms: Britain 1066-1500

Period B   The twentieth-century world

A   B

☐ ☑ Telephones are widely used.

☐ ☑ Most people work in offices, factories and shops.

☑ ☐ Sailing ships carry trade to Europe.

☑ ☐ Human labour is the most important energy source.

☑ ☐ Most people earn their living on the land.

☐ ☑ Antibiotics cure many infections.

☑ ☐ Wool is a vital industry.

☐ ☑ Petrol engines are important energy converters.

"The number you have dialled is not yet available..."

Your answers should show that you understand some of the important differences between medieval times and the present day.

4 Level 4

At Level 4, you describe the characteristic features of past societies and periods. You are able to identify changes within and across periods. Study Source 1 below, then complete the activity.

SOURCE 1 During the Black Death, the plague killed large numbers of people all over Europe. Historians estimate that the population of England fell from 3.7 million in 1348 to 2.5 million in 1377. Every village was affected.

Is it me, or are there fewer people this year?

Activity

You are a villein (peasant) who has survived the plague in a medieval village. Describe the effects of the Black Death on your daily life. You should include:

- a description of the village before and after the plague
- what it is like working the land with about 30% fewer people
- an explanation of why the price of food and animals has fallen but why the price of goods produced by skilled labour has gone up.

In your answer:

- identify the main changes which have happened
- describe the characteristic features of a peasant's life during the Middle Ages. (Check in a textbook if you don't know.)

5 Level 5

At Level 5, you distinguish between different kinds of historical change, like these below:

- William I invades and imposes a new social order (political change)
- Edward I places a 33% tax on the export of raw wool. Cloth finishing (spinning, weaving) becomes much more important in England (economic change)
- Towns grow with increases in trade (economic change)
- The Black Death ruins many villages (social change)

6+ Level 6 and above

At higher levels an understanding of chronology and time periods is assumed.

Practice question

The wool trade in medieval England

Using the sources and your own knowledge, identify changes in the wool trade between 1300 and 1450.

Study the information and documents below. List changes in the wool trade and give reasons for each.

SOURCE 1 King Edward I (1294) needs to raise money to pay for his wars with the Welsh, Scots and French. He places a 33% tax on the export of raw wool; only 2% on finished cloth.

SOURCE 2 Export of Raw Wool from England

1300	35,000 sacks
1400	19,000 sacks
1450	8,000 sacks

SOURCE 3 Export of Finished Cloth from England

1347	4,422 cloths
1368	16,000 cloths
1392	43,000 cloths
1450	54,000 cloths

It's not raw wool, it's just clothes

SOURCE 4 Edward made it easier to collect taxes by fixing one town as the centre of the wool trade. Dordrecht was chosen first; later Antwerp and Calais were used. All wool had to pass through one customs point. The town fixed from year to year was known as the Staple Town.

SOURCE 5 The English finished very little of the raw wool from their own sheep, although it was of a high quality, compared with that from Italy, for example. Flemish, Genoese and Florentine merchants bought English wool cheaply. They made large profits using the raw wool to make cloth, which sold at a much higher price. Before 1273 only 30% of English wool was made into cloth in England.

SOURCE 6 **Fulling** – Woven cloth is covered with fuller's earth and placed in shallow troughs filled with water. Men and women tread the cloth. As they work the cloth shrinks so that the lines of warp and weft become invisible.

SOURCE 7 **Fulling Mill** – Water powered paddles drove hammers which beat the cloth. People were no longer needed to tread the cloth. Mills needed to be near streams for power. Before the invention of the fulling mill, cloth was made in crowded towns because lots of people were needed for the time-consuming hard labour of fulling. Soot and smoke in towns polluted the air and damaged the cloth.

SOURCE 8 The English clothiers found it easier to finish the cloth:
- in hilly districts with fast flowing streams
- close to farms where the sheep were raised
- in the countryside rather than the town.

SOURCE 9 English clothiers bought wool, hired craftsmen and exported the finished product all over Europe. From places like Lavenham, Coggeshall, Newsham and Barton, men organised a prosperous international trade. Many clothiers grew very rich. For the first time there were wealthy Englishmen who did not depend on land for their wealth.

Relevant concepts

The question on page 6 requires an understanding of the nature of the wool trade in medieval England. The following concepts are related to this theme:

Trade	The process of buying and selling goods.
Export	Selling goods and services to other countries.
Import	Buying goods and services from other countries.
Mechanisation	Replacing a human workforce with machines.
Tax	A sum of money taken away from people by the government.
Customs duty	A tax paid by those who export or import. English merchants who exported wool were made to pay a tax to the king.
Merchants	People who earn a living by trading. The majority of people in medieval England were not merchants. They were either peasants or landowners.
Urban	A built up area, such as a town.
Rural	A countryside area.
Political	To do with how power is used, eg when governments make laws.
Economic	To do with trade and wealth.
Social	To do with how people live.
Technological	To do with machinery and energy.

Tackling the question

To tackle the question on page 6 you should take the following steps:

- read through the sources given
- make sure you understand the relevant concepts
- separate the changes that took place
- sort out which changes are political, economic, social or technological
- look for a reason why each of the changes took place.

Look carefully at the level descriptions given at the start of this chapter. When you have finished your answer, compare it with the two answers on the following pages.

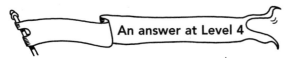

An answer at Level 4

Change in the wool trade	Reason for change
King Edward I imposed a tax on the export of wool.	The tax was 33% on raw wool, but only 2% on finished cloth.
King Edward also fixed one town as the only place from which wool could be exported abroad. It was called the Staple Town.	The first staple town was Dordrecht, followed by Antwerp and then Calais.
Raw wool exports decreased, but finished cloth exports increased.	Raw wool exports fell from 35,000 sacks in 1300 to 8,000 in 1450. Finished cloth exports rose from 4,422 cloths in 1347 to 54,000 in 1450.
The English Woollen Cloth trade became very prosperous.	They took this trade away from Flemish, Genoese and Florentine merchants. Men in places like Lavenham, Coggeshall, Newsham and Barton organised a prosperous international cloth trade.
Water powered fulling mills took over from men and women who had previously just trod the cloth.	Fulling machines were near fast flowing streams in hilly countryside areas. The water powered a hammer which beat the cloth.
The woollen cloth trade moved from the towns to the countryside.	In the countryside, the clothiers were nearer to streams and sheep farms. There was also less soot and smoke in the countryside.

Notice that the following Level 5 answer:

- gives a reason for each change rather than just describing it
- recognises the difference between political, economic, social and technological changes
- gives more detail.

This is how to improve your chronological skills.

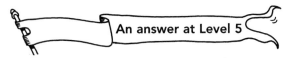

An answer at Level 5

Change in the wool trade	Reason for change
King Edward I imposed a 33% tax, or customs duty, on the export of raw wool and a 2% tax on the export of the finished cloth. (Political)	Edward needed money to fight his wars against the Welsh, Scots and French. At this time England exported a lot of raw wool, so this tax would yield a lot of extra money.
King Edward fixed one town as the only place from which English raw wool could be exported. It was called the Staple Town. (Economic)	Edward wanted to make it easy for his men to collect the new tax.
Raw wool exports decreased from 35,000 sacks in 1300 to 8,000 in 1450, but exports of finished cloth rose from 4,422 cloths in 1347 to 54,000 in 1450. (Economic)	It became harder and more expensive to export raw wool because of the system of custom duties and staple towns. It was easier and more profitable for the wool merchants to make the finished cloth in England and then export it
The Woollen Cloth trade in England became very prosperous. Wool merchants became rich men, organising their trade around towns like Lavenham, Coggeshall, Newsham and Barton, and selling to places all over Europe. (Economic)	English wool was of a higher quality than other wool and therefore so was the cloth. The quality improved further when the production of the cloth switched from the towns to the countryside because there was less pollution in the countryside. As a result, English cloth sold for a high price and was very popular.
The process of fulling was mechanised. Water power replaced human power. (Technological)	When the fulling machine was invented it took away the need to tread the cloth by foot. Fulling machines used fast flowing streams to power a hammer which beat the cloth.
The Woollen Cloth trade shifted from the urban areas to rural areas. (Social)	The new fulling machines needed fast flowing streams which were usually sited in hilly countryside areas. It was also more convenient to situate the production of cloth close to sheep farms in order to cut down on the cost of transporting the raw wool.
For the first time there were wealthy Englishmen who did not depend on the land for their wealth. (Social)	Before this time most wealth was created by owning land. Now the wealthy wool merchants were making their fortune out of trading in goods instead.

Additional questions

To test your chronological skills further, try these additional questions.

1 English kings from 1066 to 1272

When did the following kings reign over England?

From the list below, consider each king and place him in his correct position in the family tree opposite:

- Stephen (1135-1154)
- Henry II (1154-1189)
- William II 'Rufus' (1087-1100)
- John (1199-1216)
- Richard I (1189-1199)
- William I (1066-1087)
- Henry I (1100-1135)
- Henry III (1216-1272)

Stand still, while I count you...

Test your knowledge

1 How many children did William I and his wife Matilda have?

2 Henry I was king after William II. The two men were related. What was their relationship?

3 Who was Henry II's eldest son and why did he not become king?

4 Name the two sons of Henry II who did become king.

Research question

Why did Robert, the eldest son of William I, never become King?

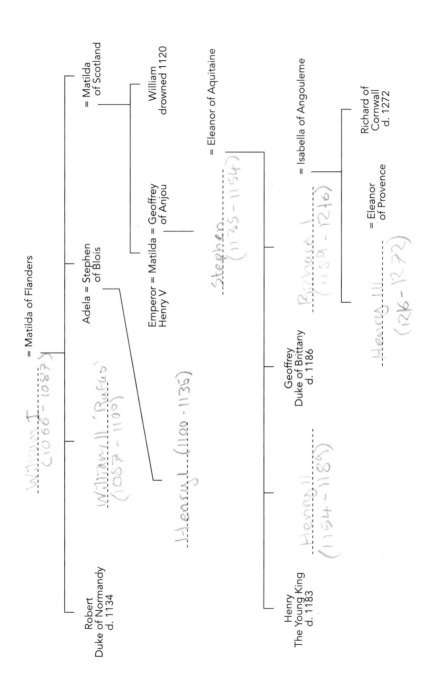

Robert
Duke of Normandy
d. 1134

William I
(1066-1087)
= Matilda of Flanders

William II 'Rufus'
(1087-1100)

Henry I (1100-1135)

= Matilda
of Scotland

William
drowned 1120

Adela = Stephen
of Blois

Emperor = Matilda = Geoffrey
Henry V   of Anjou

Stephen
(1135-1154)

= Eleanor of Aquitaine

Henry II
(1154-1189)

Henry
The Young King
d. 1183

Geoffrey
Duke of Brittany
d. 1186

Richard I
(1189-1216)

= Isabella of Angouleme

Richard of
Cornwall
d. 1272

Henry III
(126-1272)

= Eleanor
of Provence

2 The Norman Conquest

What did William change after the Norman Conquest in 1066?

When the Normans conquered England they brought with them new ideas and ways of life. Draw a chart similar to the one below and fill in the appropriate details.

	Before 1066	After 1066	Any differences?
The building of castles	motte + bailey	stone keeps + curbin walls	improvement Don't burn hard er to fnece
Organisation of the people	minimal	Areas ruled by Barons. Domesday Book	more organised easier to rule + squash rebellion
Ownership of land			
The building of churches			
Forest laws			

You must research each area and decide which remained the same and which changed after the arrival of William I in England.

William takes advantage of an English misunderstanding

3 Robin Hood

How can the legend of Robin Hood be traced to the medieval period?

Robin Hood is a popular 'folk hero' from medieval history and historians are not certain if he really existed.

In fact, historians believe Robin Hood probably lived some time in the period 1200-1400. Find out the answers to the following questions and explain why they would help historians to date Robin Hood in history.

Royal Forests

1 When and by whom, were the Royal Forests enlarged?

2 Who controlled the Royal Forests?

3 Who enforced the laws of the forests?

4 What did the people think about these people?

5 Did the people obey these laws?

Outlaws

1 Who were outlaws?

2 What had they done to be given such a title?

3 Why is Robin Hood shown as a leader of a group of outlaws?

Origins of the legend of Robin Hood

1 When did the first tales of Robin Hood appear?

2 How was the legend spread?

I'm not giving you anything until you prove you exist...

4 The Peasants' Revolt

What were the long and short term causes of the Peasants' Revolt?

The Peasants' Revolt was an important event, but what caused it to happen? Many historians agree that there were a number of reasons why the revolt occurred in 1381. They split them into two categories:

- **Long term causes** – a build up of reasons for the revolt which happened over a number of years.

- **Short term causes** – events which occurred in 1381 and were a 'spark' which caused the revolt to happen.

Look at and research the following causes of the Peasants' Revolt and create two lists of long and short term causes to explain the event.

SOURCE 1 The Black Death (1348) had killed many people so there was a shortage of labourers to tend the fields. Labourers/peasants found themselves in a strong position and could ask for higher wages.

SOURCE 2 In 1377, Richard II brought in a new tax. He needed to raise money to continue the war with France. Called the 'poll tax', it had to be paid by every person over the age of 14.

SOURCE 3 Priests such as John Ball argued that peasants deserved more rewards and that they should not have to suffer from hard work and poverty. The Archbishop of Canterbury imprisoned John Ball. People were afraid he would stir up the peasantry.

SOURCE 4 Peasants moved around the country seeking employment on the best terms they could demand.

SOURCE 5 A second 'poll tax' was introduced in 1379 and a third in 1380. The peasants did not like having to pay this tax. Their resistance led to riots and rebellion.

SOURCE 6 The Statute of Labourers tried to stop peasants from earning higher wages and tried to keep peasants in their own area. Peasants began to group together to resist officials and laws.

Timeline 1066-1500

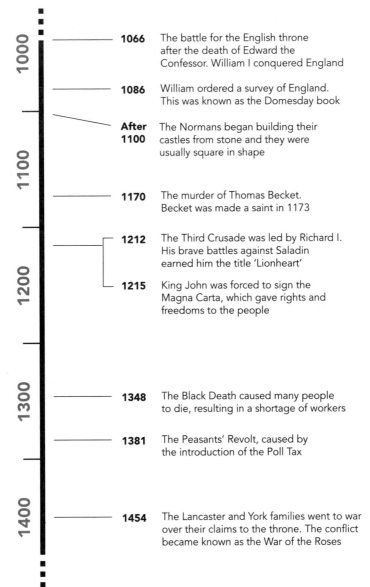

1066 The battle for the English throne after the death of Edward the Confessor. William I conquered England

1086 William ordered a survey of England. This was known as the Domesday book

After 1100 The Normans began building their castles from stone and they were usually square in shape

1170 The murder of Thomas Becket. Becket was made a saint in 1173

1212 The Third Crusade was led by Richard I. His brave battles against Saladin earned him the title 'Lionheart'

1215 King John was forced to sign the Magna Carta, which gave rights and freedoms to the people

1348 The Black Death caused many people to die, resulting in a shortage of workers

1381 The Peasants' Revolt, caused by the introduction of the Poll Tax

1454 The Lancaster and York families went to war over their claims to the throne. The conflict became known as the War of the Roses

2 Knowledge and understanding

CROWNS, PARLIAMENTS AND PEOPLES

This chapter aims to extend your knowledge and understanding of some of the political, economic, social and religious changes that shaped Britain under the Tudors and Stuarts (1500-1750). As you analyse the examples provided, you will develop your understanding of the different causes and reasons which shaped historical events during the period. You will continue to use your knowledge of chronology to understand changes in the context of time and place.

To demonstrate knowledge and understanding you:

- describe historical events and changes *(Level 1)*

- explain the reasons for, and results of, particular events and changes *(Level 2)*

- understand how political, economic, social and religious causes shape the past and have a range of consequences *(Level 3)*

- understand how a variety of causes are connected through different times and places, and that some causes are more important than others *(Level 4)*

- assess the relative significance of events, people and changes *(Level 5)*

- analyse and explain how people's ideas, beliefs and attitudes are related to the circumstances in which they find themselves. *(Level 6)*

Don't get me wrong... it's a very nice sundial but, it's a bit big, Ben...

Historians usually group causes and changes as follows:

Cause or change	Typical event, person or situation	Example
Political Actions by political leaders have lasting consequences	Change in government/law King, Political Leader Public protests; elections	English Civil War French Revolution Parliamentary Reform
Economic Natural change or human invention creates or alters patterns of jobs, wealth or poverty	Disease, famine Inventor, business man Unemployment, new social groups	Black Death, Cholera Royal grant of monopolies Invention of fulling mill; spinning-jenny, three field system
Social Groups of people, influenced by other changes, begin to live in different ways	War, persecution or economic change Men, women, particular social groups Growth of trade and towns	Norman conquest and feudalism Cotton mills and urban life in industrial England
Religious People's beliefs and attitudes shape their actions in society and politics	Religious leader or rebel preaches and publishes new ideas	Martin Luther and the Protestant Reformation

To test your understanding, tick any one box for each event/change:

Political	Economic	Social	Religious	Event/Change
☐	☑	☐	☐	London's population increases from 50,000 to 500,000 between 1500 and 1750.
☑	☐	☐	☐	Charles I decides to rule without parliament.
☐	☐	☑	☐	Landowners put hedges round open fields and pasture, forcing tenants and labourers to leave their villages.
☐	☐	☐	☑	Martin Luther publishes *The Liberty of a Christian Man* in 1520 criticising the church.

Level 3

To achieve Level 3, you must be able to give a few reasons for events and changes. Complete the activity below.

Activity

Tick the **three** reasons which you think are most important in explaining why Philip II of Spain sent his Armada against England in 1588:

- ☐ England under Elizabeth was a Protestant country.

- ☐ Spain was 100% Roman Catholic.

- ☐ John Hawkins and Francis Drake challenged Spain's right to monopolise trade in the New World.

- ☐ Philip II was anxious to crush the Protestant revolt against Spanish rule in the Netherlands.

- ☑ England and Spain tried to block each other's trade in the 1560s.

- ☑ Elizabeth sent an expeditionary force to help the Dutch Protestant rebels in 1585.

- ☐ Spain sent Catholic missionaries to England.

- ☑ Elizabeth seized Spanish gold in 1568.

4 Level 4

At Level 4, you recognise that historical events usually have more than one cause and one consequence. Enter one of the reasons from the list on page 20 into the appropriate section of this table to show you understand the rivalries which led to war.

Political	*Religious*	*Economic*
		Elizabeth siezed spanish gold in 1568

5/6 Levels 5 and 6

At this level, you are expected to examine and analyse the reasons for, and results of, events and changes. You must understand:

- different kinds of change
- different types of cause and consequence.

Activity

Consider the following factors which contributed to Henry VIII's decision to make himself head of the English Church and to push through the Reformation. In your opinion, which of these reasons are religious, political, economic or personal?

Political	Economic	Social	Religious	
☐	☐	☐	☑	William Tyndale's translation of the New Testament (1526) helped spread Protestantism in England and challenged the Roman Church.
☐	☑	☐	☐	The Pope was head of the English Church. He had authority over the clergy and the right to raise taxes.
☐	☑	☐	☐	Henry VIII fought expensive foreign wars and was eager to seize and sell church property to raise money.
☑	☐	☐	☐	Henry VIII was madly in love with Anne Boleyn and wanted to divorce his wife, Catherine of Aragon.
☑	☐	☐	☐	Henry VIII was desperate for a male heir to secure the Tudor dynasty. Catherine failed him in this respect.
☑	☐	☐	☐	Cardinal Wolsey failed to obtain from the Pope a quiet annulment of Henry's marriage; Catherine's nephew, Charles V controlled Rome.
☐	☐	☐	☑	Henry VIII supported Catholic doctrine.

7+ Levels 7, 8 and GCSE grades A* to C

At higher levels, you analyse complex causes and consequences. You explore the relative significance of events, people and changes in their wider historical context. You analyse and explain how people's ideas, belief and attitudes are related to their circumstances.

You fancy her, don't you...?

Practice question

Dissolution of the monasteries

Using the sources and your own knowledge, explain why the monasteries were dissolved.

Consider the points on page 22. Study the sources and information below. Explain why the monasteries were dissolved.

SOURCE 1 Between 1536 and 1540 Henry VIII ordered Thomas Cromwell to close down (dissolve) the monasteries.

In the years before 1536, hundreds of monks lived in a typical monastery, working the land, collecting rents from other farmers, helping the sick and the poor, educating the young and, above all, worshipping God. Many monasteries grew very rich; some did not live up to their vows to be poor.

Thomas Cromwell sent his own men (visitors) to find out how rich the monasteries were and to check the behaviour of the monks. He knew that it would be easier to close a monastery and take its wealth if there were documents appearing to prove the monks were wicked or selfish.

SOURCE 2 Simon Fish was a writer who hated priests. Like many lay people in England, he believed that priests lived well while ordinary poor people suffered:

And what do all this greedy sort of sturdy, idle, holy thieves, with these yearly exactions that they take of the people? Truly, nothing, but exempt themselves from the obedience of your Grace!... Nothing but apply themselves... to have to do with every man's wife, every man's daughter... that their bastards might inherit the possessions of every man... So take from them all these things... set these sturdy loobies abroad in the world, to get them wives of their own, to get their living with their labour in the sweat of their faces.

SOURCE 3 Extract from *Valor Ecclesiaticus* (The Wealth of the Church) 1535.

This was drafted so the crown would know what wealth the religious houses possessed. NB: At this period a labourer earned no more than a few shillings.

Temporalities
The site of the monastery of Peterborough aforesaid, with the court, gardens, orchards and divers houses... also the demesne lands, meadows and pastures   £55 3s 10d

Rents of assize with the rents and farms of tenants in divers lordships, villas, hamlets and parishes

The Lordship of Peterborough	£70 6s 8d
Eye	£63 3s 10d
Thorpe	£41 3s 10d
Castor	£34 9s 2d
Werrington	£35 19s 2d
Walton	£16 1s 8d
Glinton	£57 13s 8d

SOURCE 4 William More, Prior of Worcester
William More kept accounts of all his spending between 1518 and 1536. Here are some of the items:

Bows and arrows for hunting	3s 8d
Maidens for their singing on May day	1s 4d
Church ale and a play	7s 6d
A tonne of wine to my brother	£5
Repairing high altar at Grymley Church	4s 6d
Rewarded church clerk when robbed	12d
To Sir Thomas Edwards for lining, gilding and drawing mass books	1s
Coops, vestments, tinnacles, albes, stoles, fannells	£90
Mitre from John Cranks, goldsmith	£49
Pastoral staff	£28
Garnishing burial stone	£10

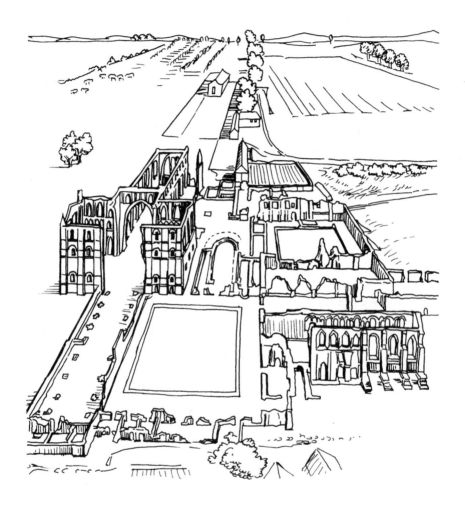

The ruins of Rievaulx today. In the 1160s it housed 140 choir monks and 500 lay brothers. The plan, with church, chapter house and dormitory, with the roofless refectory (dining room) in the foreground, followed the pattern of Cistercian houses. The Church was rebuilt in the thirteenth century. After the dissolution it became a ruin

An artist's impression of monks dining in the refectory

Relevant concepts

The question on page 24 requires an understanding of English monasteries in the sixteenth century. The following concepts are related to this theme:

Dissolution	To close down. The dissolution of the monasteries involved the state closing them down and seizing all their wealth.
Demesne	Lands owned by a lord, or in this case a monastery.
Lay people (Laity)	People who do not work for the Church.
Catholicism	A type of Christian religion. The Catholic Church is led by the Pope in Rome.
Protestantism	Another type of Christian religion. Protestantism developed from the break made from Rome by the German priest Martin Luther in 1517.

Key to the sources

The following specialist terms are used in the sources:

Assize	Local court which was managed by the monasteries.
Exactions	Money paid to the church by the laity. The author is calling them exactions because he feels they are forced out of the people.
Loobies	A slang term used to describe monks as rich, lazy and good for nothing!
Coops, vestments, tinnacles, albes, stoles, fannells and mitres	Adornments to clothing worn by clergy during religious ceremonies.
Cistercian	One of a number of religious houses. Monasteries were organised around such houses.
Pastoral staff	Staff helping the Church.

Tackling the question

To tackle the question on page 24 you should go through the following stages:

- read through all the factors which contributed to Henry VIII's decision to make himself head of the English Church and push through the Reformation

- establish which of the above reasons are political, economic, social or religious

- read carefully through all the sources on the dissolution of the monasteries

- make sure you understand the relevant concepts

- look carefully at the level descriptions given at the start of this chapter

- identify a number of reasons why Henry wanted to dissolve the monasteries.

Decide which of these was the most important reason:

- Consider which was Henry's immediate priority.

- Recognise that the real reason for doing something is often not the reason that is given to other people. Henry and Cromwell may not have been entirely honest about why they dissolved the monasteries.

- What did Henry stand to gain by doing this?

From this you will see that the most important reason is the one that mattered most to Henry.

An answer at Level 4

Notice that this answer identifies several reasons for the dissolution of the monasteries and separates them into religious, economic and political. It does not explain which were the most important reasons.

The monasteries were dissolved for several reasons. The first were religious reasons. King Henry VIII fell out with the Catholic Church because the Pope would not let him divorce his wife, Catherine of Aragon. Henry made himself Head of the Church in England. He expected people to obey him, but the monasteries were still loyal to the Roman Catholic Church.

Also, many people felt that the monasteries were too rich and extravagant. Monks and nuns were supposed to live simple lives and help the poor and sick. But some of them, like William More in Worcester, spent large sums of money on fancy clothes, wine and entertainment. Thomas Cromwell sent men round the monasteries checking up on them, and found that some of them were very large (eg Rievaulx) and very rich (eg Peterborough).

Meanwhile, King Henry had an economic reason of his own for dissolving the monasteries. He was very short of money after fighting some expensive wars. He and Cromwell realised that if they took over the monasteries and sold off their lands, they could raise a lot of money.

Finally, Henry had a political reason too. He was a very proud, ambitious king who wanted more power for himself. He wanted to get rid of the monasteries because they were still loyal to the Pope in Rome. Then he would have power over the whole of the Church in England.

Do you have a club card Mr More?

An answer at Level 6

Notice that this answer makes it clear right from the start what was the most important reason for the dissolution of the monasteries. It also makes it clear how the different types of causes link together. This is why it is better than the Level 4 answer.

The monasteries were dissolved by King Henry VIII between 1536 and 1540. With the help of his chief minister, Thomas Cromwell, he took over their lands and wealth and sold them off for a large profit. The reasons for the dissolution of the monasteries were political, religious and economic, but I think the economic reasons were the most important.

Henry had built up large debts from fighting a series of expensive foreign wars during his reign. In order to maintain his power, he needed to raise money without creating too many enemies. The dissolution of the monasteries was the ideal solution. The monasteries were very wealthy but they were defenceless. They were an easy target. This is why Henry instructed Cromwell to carry out the dissolution.

The dissolution was made easier for Henry because the monasteries had become very unpopular. Monks and nuns were supposed to live simple lives and help the poor and sick, but some of them had become very rich and extravagant with money forced out of lay people. For example, the account book of William More, Prior of Worcester, shows that he spent large sums of money on ceremonial clothing, wine and entertainment. The ruins of the monastery at Rievaulx show that it was a huge place with room for over 600 people. When Thomas Cromwell carried out a survey of the monasteries in the *Valor Ecclesiasticus*, he found that many monasteries had extensive lands and income. For example, the monastery at Peterborough had land worth over £55 and collected rents of over £70, which were large sums of money in those days.

However, we must be careful with such sources because Cromwell may have exaggerated the figures to make the monasteries look richer than they were. It was easier for Henry to dissolve the monasteries if they were unpopular. Some people were already very critical of the monks. For example, Simon Fish wrote that monks were "sturdy, idle, holy thieves" who ought to be made to work for their living. Perhaps Fish was a Protestant and wanted to make the Catholic Church look bad. Protestantism had been growing in England and Henry himself quarrelled with the Pope over his divorce from Catherine of Aragon. Henry was quite happy to stir up anti-Catholic feeling among the Protestants. So although religious disagreements were not the main reason for the dissolution of the monasteries, they helped to make it popular in England.

Finally, Henry may have had it at the back of his mind that the monasteries were more loyal to the Pope than to him. Henry had already shown that he was an ambitious and determined man, who wanted power over the whole country. Now that he was on bad terms with the Pope, he was afraid that the monasteries might cause trouble for him. He may therefore have been glad to see the back of the monasteries, especially if it made him more popular with the people.

In conclusion, the dissolution of the monasteries took place because Henry badly needed money and the monasteries were an easy target. Religious and political reasons were also important, but the economic reason was the main one which persuaded Henry that the dissolution of the monasteries was the best thing to do.

Additional questions

To develop your knowledge and understanding skills, try the following questions relating to the Tudor and Stuart periods.

 ## 1 The Elizabethan Poor

Why did the poor become a problem during the reign of Elizabeth I?

Historians list a number of reasons why the number of people living in poverty increased.

Look at the following reasons and decide whether each is a political, economic, social or religious reason:

- The number of people in England was rising and there were not enough jobs to go round.

- Monasteries had given help to the poor but had been closed by Henry VIII (between 1536-1540).

- Bad harvests had pushed up the price of food. Food was expensive.

- Wages remained low whilst prices rose steadily.

- Many farmers 'enclosed' their land. They stopped growing crops and kept sheep instead. Fewer labourers were needed to look after sheep.

Now use your knowledge and understanding of the reasons why the poor had become a problem to answer the question.

2 The Gunpowder Plot

What happened on 5 November 1605?

Write a newspaper article dated 6 November 1605 that tells of the events which occurred two nights ago. You are a Catholic and therefore you must write your article from this point of view.

Consider the following questions, and respond to them as if you were a Catholic. This will help you understand and explain the reasons for the Gunpowder Plot:

- How do you feel about James I? Do you support him as the King?

- What are your thoughts about James' actions when he asked Roman Catholic priests to leave the country?

- What do you want the King to do about the religious problems?

- Do you know Robert Catesby and Thomas Percy? Have you been given any 'inside' information about the plot?

- What details do you know about the plot and what happened on the evening of the 4 November 1605?

- Are you pleased that the plot was stopped just in time?

Now write your newspaper article. This will test your ability to use your knowledge and assess the historical evidence.

'Light blue touch paper and retire...'

3 The English Civil War – 1

What were the differences between the Battles of Edgehill and Naseby?

Explain the differences between the fighting experience at two major battles in the Civil War: the Battle of Edgehill in 1642 and the Battle of Naseby in 1645.

To help you, research the following questions and perhaps draw up a list of the differences before you answer the question:

- What type of soldiers fought in the war? What did Pikemen, Musketeers and the Cavalry actually do? What role did they have during the battles?

- What training did the soldiers receive? How were they organised?

- Did the fighting experience differ for Roundheads and Cavaliers?

- What role did Oliver Cromwell play in the Civil War and particularly at the Battle of Naseby in 1645?

- Was the King a good leader of his army?

- Which side won the battles at Edgehill and Naseby?

Now use your knowledge and understanding of the battles to answer the question.

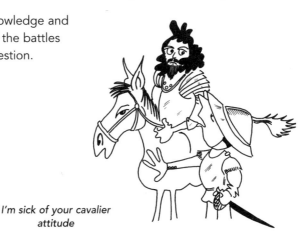

I'm sick of your cavalier attitude

4 The English Civil War – 2

Why did Parliament and the Roundheads eventually win the Civil War?

Historians have listed a number of reasons for Parliament's victory.

You are a young historian and your task is to assess three reasons for Parliament winning. Use your knowledge to research the following arguments and decide which reason you consider to be the **most important**. Remember you must support your answer with evidence based on your understanding of the events of the Civil War.

Reason for Parliament winning the Civil War include:

- The Roundheads had the support of traders in the south-east. They had the money to pay for the war.

- The Navy supported Parliament. They protected various ports around the country.

- Oliver Cromwell was the main force behind the Roundheads because of his creation of the New Model Army.

Timeline 1500-1750

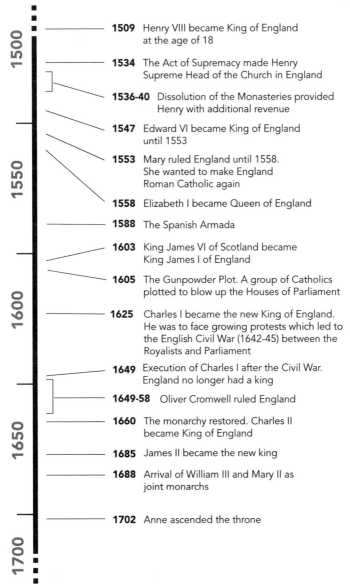

1509 Henry VIII became King of England at the age of 18

1534 The Act of Supremacy made Henry Supreme Head of the Church in England

1536-40 Dissolution of the Monasteries provided Henry with additional revenue

1547 Edward VI became King of England until 1553

1553 Mary ruled England until 1558. She wanted to make England Roman Catholic again

1558 Elizabeth I became Queen of England

1588 The Spanish Armada

1603 King James VI of Scotland became King James I of England

1605 The Gunpowder Plot. A group of Catholics plotted to blow up the Houses of Parliament

1625 Charles I became the new King of England. He was to face growing protests which led to the English Civil War (1642-45) between the Royalists and Parliament

1649 Execution of Charles I after the Civil War. England no longer had a king

1649-58 Oliver Cromwell ruled England

1660 The monarchy restored. Charles II became King of England

1685 James II became the new king

1688 Arrival of William III and Mary II as joint monarchs

1702 Anne ascended the throne

1500 1550 1600 1650 1700

3 Interpretations of history

This chapter helps you understand how and why events, people and situations have been interpreted differently. Major changes, like the overthrow of the monarchy in France and the development of the factory system in Britain, provoked strong reactions. People at the time, and historians since, have argued about what happened. Was the result of the French Revolution freedom or murder? Did cotton mills improve or worsen the lives of the new working class? You will study examples from National Curriculum Study Unit 3 which show how writers have selected evidence to suit their interpretations.

Consider an example.

When factory owners introduced power looms (c1785) the impact was dramatic. Home-based hand loom weavers despaired because they could not compete with machinery. Poverty followed and their way of life disappeared. But factories produced more cloth and profits rose. Prosperous mill towns developed. Long hours were worked, often in unsafe conditions.

Your interpretation of these simple facts would depend on the factors outlined in the following table:

Oh, and 6,000 eclairs on Marie Antoinette's account...

Your point of view	Your ideas about society	Where you live or places you choose to study	Time period commented on	Sources selected
Hand loom weaver	Like old-fashioned village life; value your own skills	In a village; since power looms came in everyone has suffered	When income has reached rock bottom	Personal experience; comments of neighbours
Mill owner	Profit should guide action	Comfortable house far from factory	When competition with other factories is squeezing profits	Business accounts at this period
Factory worker	Regular factory wages are better than starvation	New house near factory	When factory is taking on new staff and wages are good	Personal experience; comments of neighbours
Economic analyst	Economic progress is inevitable; everyone benefits in the end	In London; never seen industry in action	1780s: Britain's trade and output are rising fast	National accounts of trade and industry
Newspaper critic looking for 'news'	People become slaves in factories	Visiting districts where there are protests and demonstrations	After the Napoleonic wars when discontent is at a peak	Interviews with people short of work and food

Interpretations of history

To recognise and understand different interpretations of the past you:

- distinguish between a fact and a point of view *(Level 1)*
- understand how gaps in the available evidence may lead to different interpretations *(Level 2)*
- are aware that interpretations of the past may differ from what is known to have happened *(Level 3)*
- demonstrate how historical interpretations depend on the selection of sources *(Level 4)*
- describe the strengths and weaknesses of different interpretations of an historical event or development *(Level 5)*
- show how attitudes and circumstances can influence an individual's interpretation of events. *(Level 6)*

Level 3

At Level 3, you know the difference between a fact and a point of view. Consider the source below from the French *Archives Nationales*, May 1793:

> **SOURCE** The aristocrat is a man who, because of his scorn or indifference, has not been entered on the register of National Guards, and who has not taken the civic oath... He is a man who, by his conduct as well as by his connections, has given proof that he bitterly regrets the passing of the ancient regime and despises every aspect of the Revolution. He is a man whose conduct suggests that he would send cash to the emigrés or join the enemy army...

Does this account of *the aristocrat* represent a fair, factual description of the French aristocracy during the Revolution? What type of person might have written the account? Suggest motives for describing aristocrats like this.

Level 4

At Level 4, you understand that limited evidence may lead to different interpretations. A number of detailed studies have shown that the standard of living improved during the Industrial Revolution. Other sources support the argument that ordinary people suffered hard times because of economic change.

Level 5

At Level 5, you recognise that some interpretations, including popular accounts, may differ from what is known to have happened. Complete the activity below.

Activity

Consider the following points:

- During the eighteenth century, The Bastille never held more than 40 prisoners. When it was stormed on 14 July, 1789 there were six prisoners.

- Only 100 people were killed during the fighting. Entry was achieved by negotiation.

- The Storming of the Bastille has been celebrated throughout France as a major national event ever since.

Use the following points to explain why the capture of the Bastille has been interpreted as a major event despite the limited scale of the fighting and the even more limited strategic significance of the Bastille itself.

- Famous critics of l'Ancien Régime (eg Voltaire, Linguet) were imprisoned in the Bastille.

- The Bastille was associated with the hated lettres de cachet, used by the King to authorise the arrest and indefinite detention of his opponents.

- Bread prices nearly doubled in the period immediately before the fall of the Bastille. Louis XVI was extremely unpopular.

- News came on 12 July 1789 that hard-liners, who wanted to crush the Revolution by force, had persuaded the King to sack Necker, his moderate, reforming minister.

- The Bastille had achieved mythical status as a symbol of Royal power.

 Level 6

To achieve Level 6, you demonstrate how interpretations depend on the selection of sources.

Positive accounts of Napoleon select sources which:

- Illustrate his efforts to consolidate the Revolution.

- Detail his administrative and legislative achievements (Code Napoleon).

- Show how he defended France's natural frontiers against her enemies.

- Demonstrate his genius as a military commander.

Negative accounts of Napoleon select sources which:

- Reveal Napoleon as a ruthless opportunist concerned only with power.

- Show his domestic reforms as dictatorial, conservative and geared to strengthening France as a war machine.

- Indicate that he fought out of ambition; that he sacrificed the French to the greater glory of Napoleon.

- Emphasise his mistakes (especially at Borodino, Moscow and Waterloo) and the high cost of victory and defeat.

… and who shall I be today?

 ## Levels 7, 8 and GCSE grades A* to C

At higher levels, you describe the strengths and weaknesses of different interpretations of an historical event or development (see the practice question overpage). You show how attitudes and circumstances can influence an individual's interpretation of events. You analyse and explain various interpretations of the past.

Practice question

The Peterloo 'Massacre', 16 August 1819

Using the sources below, explain what are the strengths and weaknesses of each of the following interpretations.

Interpretation 1: E P Thompson

- Peterloo really was a massacre.

- The presence of large numbers of women and children show the peaceful intentions of the reformers.

- Manchester manufacturers, merchants, publicans and shop keepers were driven by class hatred.

- Lord Liverpool declared that the action of the Manchester magistrates was right and that there was no alternative but to support them.

- The government acted swiftly and vigorously, using every resource to ensure the reformers were crushed.

Interpretation 2: Donald Read

- The Tory government was not repressive like those in Russia or Austria.

- Lord Liverpool's government did not desire or cause the events at St Peter's Fields, Manchester.

- Home Office policy was peaceful; the Manchester magistrates were to blame.

SOURCE 1 news report in *The Times*, 19 August, 1819

Within 20 minutes of the commencement of the meeting, the Yeomanry Cavalry of the town of Manchester charged the populace sword in hand, cut their way to the platform, and with the police at their head, made prisoners of Hunt and several of those who surrounded him – seized the flags of the Reformers – trampled down and cut down a number of the people, who, after throwing some stones and brickbats at the cavalry in its advance towards the hustings, fled on all sides in the utmost confusion and dismay. Of the crowd... a large portion consisted of women. About eight or ten persons were killed, and, besides those whom their friends carried off, above 50 wounded were taken to the hospitals; but the gross number is not supposed to have fallen short of 80 or 100, more or less, grievously wounded.

Was that (meeting) at Manchester an 'unlawful assembly'? Was the notice of it unlawful? We believe not. Was the subject proposed for discussion (a reform in the House of Commons) an unlawful object? Assuredly not. Was anything done at this meeting before the cavalry rode in upon it, either contrary to law or in breach of the peace? No such circumstance is recorded in any of the statements which have yet reached our hands.

SOURCE 2 The Manchester magistrates report to Lord Sidmouth on the evening of Peterloo

There was no appearance of arms or pikes, but great plenty of sticks and staves... Long before... (Hunt's arrival) the magistrates had felt a decided conviction that the array was such as to terrify all the King's subjects, and was such as no legitimate purpose could justify... While the cavalry was forming, a most marked defiance of them was acted by the reforming part of the mob.

What? They started it!

SOURCE 3 Lord Liverpool to Canning, 23 September, 1819

When I say that the proceedings of the magistrates at Manchester were justifiable, you will understand me as not by any means deciding that the course which they pursued on that occasion was in all its part prudent. A great deal might be said in their favour even on his head; but, whatever judgement might be formed in this respect, being satisfied that they were substantially right, there remained no alternative but to support them.

SOURCE 4 Canning's View

To let down the magistrates would be to invite their resignations and to lose all gratuitous service in the counties liable to disturbance for ever. It is, to be sure, very provoking that the magistrates, right as they were in principle, and nearly right in practice, should have spoilt the completeness of their case by half an hour's precipitation.

Relevant concepts

The practice question ob page 44 requires an understanding of the campaign to reform parliament in the early nineteenth century. The following concepts are related to this theme:

Reformers	Those who called for a change in the political system, eg to grant the vote to all adult men. Only one in 20 adult men could vote at this time.

All those in favour...motion carried

Repression	Putting down rivals. The government was accused of using force to put down the reformers, for example, by preventing them from having free speech. Critics of the government accused it of repression at Peterloo.
Revolution	A process of complete change. A political revolution would involve the government being overthrown, perhaps violently. The government in 1819 was afraid of a revolution, especially if a large crowd of reformers met.
Class hatred	The middle classes owned property and most of them were employers. Some employers paid their workers badly and made them work in difficult conditions. This caused some workers to feel quite angry. The result was class hatred. It also made the middle classes fear a workers' rebellion.

Tackling the question

To tackle the question on page 44 you should go through the following stages:

- read through the sources carefully
- find out as much information as you can from other sources on the Peterloo massacre
- make sure you understand the relevant concepts
- work out *why* the interpretations differ before deciding on their strengths and weaknesses
- look carefully at the level descriptions given at the start of this chapter.

How to work out the strengths and weaknesses of an interpretation:

- A strength is an aspect of an interpretation that can be backed up by other evidence.
- A weakness is an aspect of an interpretation that is in conflict with other evidence.

An answer at Level 5

Notice that this answer describes **how** the interpretations differ and also why they differ but only gives a very general conclusion on the strengths and weaknesses of the interpretations. The sources are not really used and there is little evidence of the pupil's own knowledge.

Thompson thinks that Peterloo was a massacre. He takes the side of the ordinary people who went to the meeting at St Peter's Fields and sees everything from their point of view. He says that a lot of women and children went to the meeting, which shows that they did not plan to be violent. They were trying to run away when the cavalry attacked them. Thompson says that the rich people in Manchester, like manufacturers and shopkeepers, were driven by class hatred and acted violently against the crowd. He also blamed the Government for supporting the magistrates and crushing the reformers.

Read disagrees with this. He points out that it was the Manchester magistrates and not the Government which ordered the cavalry to attack the crowd. He says that governments in some other countries like Austria and Russia were much worse than in England. He describes the policy of the Government as 'peaceful', so the Manchester magistrates must take all the blame.

Thompson's interpretation is good at showing how the people who went to St Peter's Fields must have felt, especially if they really were innocent. Even Read does not say that the crowd was violent. Read is good at pointing out that we should not automatically blame the Government, though Thompson shows that Lord Liverpool was quick to support the magistrates' actions. I think that the magistrates panicked when a very large crowd gathered and it was wrong and unfair of them to massacre the people.

An answer at Level 8

Notice that this answer compares the interpretations carefully with the other sources of information given and knowledge gathered through the pupil's own research. Each interpretation is examined closely before a final conclusion is reached on which is the most accurate.

The interpretations of Thompson and Read both contain some elements of the truth. On the balance of the evidence, it seems to me that the magistrates acted more brutally than they needed to and so it is right to call Peterloo a 'massacre'.

Thompson's interpretation supports this view, and there is a lot of evidence to back up his opinion. The report in *The Times* says that the cavalry charged the crowd with swords in their hands, although the crowd had done nothing to provoke the attack. They had met peacefully to discuss a perfectly lawful question, namely the reform of the House of Commons, and the meeting had only been going on for 20 minutes. Some historians, like Briggs, point out that the crowd of 50,000 was a very large one, and it is not surprising that the Manchester magistrates were alarmed. They justified their actions by saying that the 'array was such as to terrify all the King's subjects', that the crowd showed a 'marked defiance' towards the cavalry, and that they were armed with 'plenty of sticks and staves'. However, no other source contains evidence that the crowd threatened to cause violence, and it is possible that the sticks and staves were just the normal tools of working men and not weapons at all.

There is evidence that the magistrates had received many letters from the local business community urging them to ban the meeting. The magistrates were mostly members of the business community themselves, and were responsible for law and order in Manchester. They were probably afraid that thousands of angry protesters would get out of control and riot, attacking employers and their property. This is perhaps why Thompson thought that 'class hatred' was involved.

Thompson's interpretation is even backed by the statement of the Prime Minister, Lord Liverpool. He said that the behaviour of the magistrates was not 'in all its part prudent', though he had no alternative but to support them. The reason why is given by his Cabinet colleague, Canning, who explains that if the Government 'let down' these magistrates, then nobody would ever volunteer to do the job again. However, he shows that he was also unhappy with the way the Manchester magistrates had behaved. He called it 'half an hour's precipitation', suggesting that he thought they had lost their heads, and says that they were 'nearly right in practice', which actually means they were wrong!

Thompson seems to see things entirely from the point of view of the ordinary people and does not think that maintaining law and order was important. He also blamed the Government for the massacre. It is true that there was a great deal of poverty in the year 1819 and the Government was afraid that the people might start a revolution. However, Read points out that the Tory Government in Britain was not nearly as harsh and violent towards the ordinary people as the rulers of Austria or Russia. Also, there is no evidence that the Government ordered the Manchester magistrates to send in the cavalry and break up the demonstration. Maybe Read is a little too kind to the Government because they could have spoken out against the killings and shown some sympathy for the people. They had recently passed the Corn Laws which raised bread prices and made the poor even poorer.

In conclusion, I think that Thompson is right that Peterloo was a massacre against the ordinary people, but Read is right that the Government did not order it. They both say that it was a tragic accident caused by the Manchester magistrates panicking and over-reacting, and I agree with that too.

Additional questions

To explore further interpretations of the past and to develop your skills in this area, try the following questions.

1 The Atlantic Slave Trade

How is the slave trade interpreted?

How would you interpret the slave trade in the eighteenth century? Would it depend on your background and beliefs? To understand the different viewpoints towards the slave trade, imagine you are:

a   Living in Bristol in the 1750s. You own one of the many slave ships that are involved in the slave trade. Write a letter to your local newspaper showing your opinions about the slave trade and your attitude towards black people.

b   A black slave who has just arrived in America to work on one of the many sugar plantations. Write a diary entry and describe your journey on the slave ship from Africa. What are your feelings towards the people who run the slave trade and how you see your future?

Now compare the accounts. How do they differ? Find comparisons relating to:

- the opinion of black people
- the economics of the slave trade.

Now consider the following question:

- Why is it important for historians to consider a number of interpretations of the same event?

2 Agricultural Revolution 1750-1900

What changes in agriculture took place during this period?

Interpretations of events vary due to the vast numbers of people living different lifestyles.

Consider the following case study:

CASE STUDY It is 1750. John is a farmer. He has to support his wife and family solely from what he can produce on his small area of land. John has learnt various techniques from his father and uncles, who have all earned their living from farming, but is now aware that many changes are taking place within the agrarian economy. How will these changes affect John and his family?

Now consider the following years and explain how John's life would be different in each: 1750, 1800, 1850, 1900.

What would John think about the changes that were taking place in agriculture? John's thoughts are in themselves an interpretation of the past.

3   Napoleon Bonaparte 1799-1802

How would you describe Napoleon?

In 1799, Napoleon seized power in France, but what do historians think about the man and his methods of achieving dominance?

Use your knowledge and additional research to build up evidence to illustrate each of the following interpretations of Napoleon:

- He was an impressive leader of military men.
- He was a devious and clever manipulator.
- He was a risk-taker.
- He was a supporter of the Catholic Church.
- He was a brilliant Emperor.

Consider each opinion and its evidence and decide which description you believe best summarises Napoleon. Remember you must always give a reason for your answer.

An additional interpretation of Napoleon can be achieved by looking at the various paintings that are completed during this period, many of which were commissioned by Napoleon himself.

- What interpretations do the paintings give?

Would the real Napoleon please stand up...

4   The Industrial Revolution

Who was the most influential inventor during the Industrial Revolution?

The Industrial Revolution saw huge changes and was a period of new ideas and innovations. Explain the changes brought about by each of the following inventors:

- Abraham Darby (iron)
- James Watt (steam engines)
- John Kay (flying shuttle)
- James Hargreaves (spinning-jenny)
- Richard Arkwright (waterwheel)
- Samuel Crompton ('mule')
- Thomas Telford (roads)
- John Macadam (roads)
- George Stephenson (railways)
- Isambard Kingdom Brunel (railways)

Decide which inventor you think was the most important during the Industrial Revolution. Your answer will be your interpretation.

Share your thoughts in a group and consider each other's ideas. You will be aware that many different interpretations of the past exist.

...and the winner is...

Timeline 1750-c1900

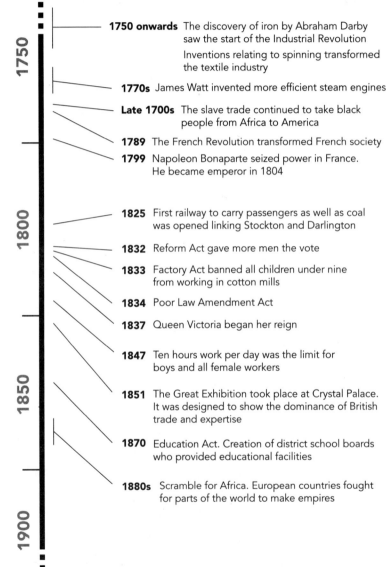

1750 onwards The discovery of iron by Abraham Darby saw the start of the Industrial Revolution

Inventions relating to spinning transformed the textile industry

1770s James Watt invented more efficient steam engines

Late 1700s The slave trade continued to take black people from Africa to America

1789 The French Revolution transformed French society

1799 Napoleon Bonaparte seized power in France. He became emperor in 1804

1825 First railway to carry passengers as well as coal was opened linking Stockton and Darlington

1832 Reform Act gave more men the vote

1833 Factory Act banned all children under nine from working in cotton mills

1834 Poor Law Amendment Act

1837 Queen Victoria began her reign

1847 Ten hours work per day was the limit for boys and all female workers

1851 The Great Exhibition took place at Crystal Palace. It was designed to show the dominance of British trade and expertise

1870 Education Act. Creation of district school boards who provided educational facilities

1880s Scramble for Africa. European countries fought for parts of the world to make empires

1750
1800
1850
1900

4 Historical enquiry

This chapter introduces the main themes and concepts you need to understand to answer questions about the causes, events and results of the wars fought between 1914-1918 and 1939-1945. As you work through the text, you will be encouraged to explore a variety of sources to develop, in particular, the skills of historical enquiry. You will continue to apply skills improved by earlier chapters.

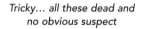

To conduct an historical enquiry you:

- collect and record information about a topic

- find out what happened using information you are given

Tricky... all these dead and no obvious suspect

- research your own information

- ask questions and answer them using information

- comment on the usefulness of information you have found

- explain how pieces of information fit into the topic.

Historical information comes from sources which include:

- books written at the time or later, including textbooks (eg *All Quiet on the Western Front*)

- other printed material, including documents, the originals of which may have been handwritten (eg *Treaty of Versailles*)

- artefacts, ie objects made from raw materials at the time or later (eg gas mask)

- drawings, photographs, films, maps (eg newsreel footage)

- buildings and sites (eg War Museum).

Level 3

To achieve Level 3, you must be able to answer simple questions by finding relevant pieces of information in a source. Study Source 1 below:

SOURCE 1 By the early months of 1917 food was becoming scarce in the towns. The German submarine campaign was taking a very heavy toll of ships bringing food to Britain. In the early weeks of 1917 it was even impossible to find potatoes in the towns. Some families could get none for a week at a time. If the shops had potatoes, the police were called in to control the hungry crowds who queued for them.

W G Hoskins, *Devon and Its People*, 1959

Questions about this source could include:

- When did food become scarce in towns?
- Why was food scarce?
- Why were police needed?

Level 4

At Level 4, you show you can select and combine information from several sources. Source 2 provides information on food during the 1914 - 1918 war:

SOURCE 2 Weekly rations in 1918:

20 ozs of meat	8 ozs of sugar
2 ozs of lard	8 ozs of bacon
	5 ozs of butter

Test questions prompt you to select information from both sources and draw conclusions:

- What was the impact of the German submarine campaign on food supplies in Britain during 1917?

- Which of the food items mentioned in Source 1 or 2 was least available?

Levels 5 and 6

Beyond Level 4, you must understand whether a source is:

- **Relevant** – How far does the information help you understand the historical topic or events you are studying? Is it important or trivial?

- **Reliable** – Who wrote the source? An eye-witness? Or was it written years later? How do we know if it is true? Does it check out with other sources?

- **Biased** – From whose point of view is the source written, eg German or British? Is it a soldier's letter describing real experience? Or is it a report written by a general to influence politicians at home?

Look at Source 3:

SOURCE 3

Richmond Barracks, Dublin
7 August 1914

My dearest Mother, Sisters and Brother

You know that we go to war on Sunday, we go into Belgium, we are fighting the Germans. It cannot last very long, not more than six months. Of course, we never know if we will return but we trust in God to spare us, some must be killed, but we'll die a credit to our country...

From your loving Son George

What are the strengths and weaknesses of this source in relation to the following historical enquiries?

- attitudes of soldiers before they went to war
- changing attitudes of soldiers towards the war
- British society and values before 1914
- military expectations of the course of the war.

Dear Mum... I hope no-one reads this in years to come...

Levels 7, 8 and GCSE grades A* to C

At higher levels you work independently. You find information for yourself, seeking out sources available in libraries and museums. You ask and answer your own questions about the sources you identify. You pick out important points. You draw your own conclusions about the topics you are asked to study. You write a careful account, supporting your conclusions with evidence drawn from a range of sources.

Practice question

What was it like in the trenches?

Using the sources and your own knowledge, explain what is meant by the term 'trench warfare' and why it led to such huge losses. What were conditions in the trenches like and how did the soldiers react to them?

Apply the skills of historical enquiry, which you have explored and practised earlier in this chapter, to investigate the information contained in the sources below.

Introduction

The war lasted over four years. The Western Front stretched from the Belgian coast to the Swiss border. It consisted of a series of trenches on each side. In some places, the Allied trenches were only 100 metres from the German ones.

For three years before the final offensive the Western Front did not shift more than about 10 miles each way as the Allies tried to push Germany out of northern France and Belgium, which the Germans had captured in the first months of the war.

The British attack on the Somme (July 1916) cost 60,000 casualties on the first day. The German's last offensive (March 1918) nearly succeeded but by November the country was exhausted and ready for peace.

SOURCE 1 Trenches were usually about two metres deep with a wooden duckboard running along the bottom to keep the troops' feet out of the mud and water that collected in the 'sump' at the bottom.

SOURCE 2 Trenches were dug in a zigzag and not in straight lines. This made them harder to capture. If one end of a trench was occupied by the enemy, they could not simply fire down the whole length of the trench.

SOURCE 3 To attack meant soldiers 'going over the top': they left their trenches and ran towards the enemy. The enemy tried to mow them down with machine-gun fire. Some just drowned in the mud.

SOURCE 4 In wet weather, and especially in Flanders in Belgium, the water and mud would often cover the soldiers' feet, leading to 'trench foot'. This meant that the soldiers' feet went numb. Amputation of toes or the whole foot might follow. During the course of the war 75,000 British troops were admitted to hospital with trench foot or frost bite. To prevent this, troops had to change into dry socks every day and rub foul smelling whale oil into their feet to act as a waterproofing agent. The officers made sure this was done because some men welcomed trench foot as a way to be invalided home, out of the war.

When did you last have an oil change?

SOURCE 5 In between attacks, men lived in these trenches. Rats swam in the water at the bottom; lice bred in the men's uniforms. Day after day, the trenches were shelled, while the rifle fire of snipers caught those who were careless. There was little time for sleep or for changing clothes. Food was often late arriving, or cold.

SOURCE 6 Trench activity increased at night. Small patrols were sent out into no-man's-land under cover of darkness. They attempted to discover details about enemy resources and strength. To guard against night-time raids both sides kept men on sentry duty and regularly lit up the sky with star shells.

SOURCE 7 You stand in a trench of vile stinking mud
And the bitter cold wind freezes your blood
Then the guns open up and flames light the sky
And, as you watch, rats go scuttling by.

The men in dugouts are quiet for a time
Trying to sleep midst the stench and the slime
The moon is just showing from over the hill
And the dead on the wire hang silent and still.

A sniper's bullet wings close to your head
As you wistfully think of a comfortable bed
But now a dirty blanket has to suffice
And more often than not it is crawling with lice.

Written by Sidney Chaplin,
Gloucestershire Regiment

SOURCE 8 We formed into one line and walked slowly forward. We had only gone a few yards when my mate, Billy Booth, was hit. Then the man on my left fell against me. Lines of men were just disappearing. The Germans' machine guns fired at us like it was target practice.

The wire was 60 yards away but only a few made it as far as that. They became fastened on the barbs and the machine guns tore their bodies to shreds. It was all over in ten minutes.

It was an absolute fiasco. A slaughter. The best of our generation died there. That's why the country hasn't been the same since. The commanders didn't care about us. I don't think they bothered about human life.

George Morgan was 18 when he fought
at the Battle of the Somme in 1916

Relevant concepts

The practice question on page 61 requires a good understanding of the nature of the fighting on the Western Front. The following concepts are related to this theme:

Attrition	Wearing down the enemy gradually. Exhausting their resources over a long period of time.
Typhus	Diseases were common in the trenches because of the filthy conditions. Rats and lice were able to breed freely, and spread diseases wherever they roamed. Typhus was one such disease.
Disillusionment	The war had started on a wave of enthusiasm. Most soldiers believed it would be a short war. However, as the war went on this feeling was replaced by bitterness and hopelessness. Many men lost faith in their leaders and began to question the whole point of the war.
Desertion	For some men the strains of war became too much and they left the front without permission. By 1917, thousands of men were deserting the British army. Even greater numbers deserted the French and Russian armies.
Mutiny	The officers in all armies kept very strict discipline. Sometimes, men were shot for desertion or cowardice. As the losses mounted, some men decided to take revenge on their officers. Orders were disobeyed and, in some instances, officers were attacked. A full scale mutiny could involve an entire company rebelling against their officers. By 1917, large sections of the Russian army were in open mutiny against their officers. The punishment for mutiny was usually execution.

No-man's-land | The area of land that separated the trenches was known as no-man's-land because it was such a dangerous place to be in. Attacks came across no-man's-land. It was often incredibly muddy and filled with craters created by shells.

Reconnaissance | Missions to gather information about the enemy's position. Aeroplanes would fly over enemy trenches to take photos and men sometimes went on night-time trips into no-man's-land to find out what the enemy were doing.

Trench foot | A severe condition caused by standing in water or mud for long periods of time. Thousands of men suffered from this condition during the course of the war.

Trench warfare | Both sides faced one another across no-man's-land in dug out trenches. Attacks were made by huge numbers of charging infantry, armed with rifles and bayonets, against an enemy trench defended with barbed wire and machine guns. The defenders had the overwhelming advantage and attacks usually resulted in huge losses and little gain.

After you Sarge!

Shelling

Before an infantry attack, artillery (big guns) was used to fire explosives into the enemy trench to clear the way for the attack. It had the disadvantage of warning the enemy that an attack was coming, and churning up no-man's-land so that it was difficult for the attacking troops to cross it.

Shell shock

Some men became so disturbed by the experience of trench warfare that they suffered from symptoms such as trembling, sweats and frequent nightmares. Some kept imagining they were still in the trenches a long time after they had left. This condition was known as shell shock.

Stalemate

The war gave a huge advantage to the defenders of trenches and attacks seemed almost pointless. Between 1914-1917 there was very little change in the overall positions of the armies on the Western Front. Neither side seemed to know how to make a breakthrough.

Whose turn is it?

Tackling the question

To tackle the question on page 61 you should take the following steps:

- read through the sources given

- make sure you understand the relevant concepts

- find out more information about the Western Front from other sources

- look carefully at the level descriptions given at the start of this chapter.

Once you have done this, you are ready to construct your answer.

An answer at Level 5

This answer would receive a Level 5 mark because it covers most of the relevant points, but includes little original research. It doesn't question the reliability of the evidence and fails to reach a conclusion.

Trench warfare was the type of warfare that developed on the Western Front during the First World War. It involved two armies digging trenches about two metres deep to protect the soldiers from enemy fire. The trenches were defended by machine guns and rows of barbed wire. Then the armies sat facing each other across an area known as no-man's-land. An attack involved 'going over the top' of your own trench and charging across no-man's-land to try to capture the enemy's trench. The attackers could be easily seen and shot down and thousands of them were killed like that. 60,000 British troops died on the first day of the Battle of the Somme, and $^3/_4$ million altogether in the War.

The reason for so many men dying was that the army leaders kept on trying the same tactics over and over again, even though they did not work. The leaders did not trust new weapons at first, like the tank, and so they did not use them much. Also they did things like ordering an artillery barricade before an attack was launched. This warned the enemy that an attack was coming and churned up the ground so that it was impossible to run or even crawl across. Some men even drowned in the mud. Maybe the generals did not have any other choices, but it made ordinary soldiers like George Morgan, aged 18, think that 'the commanders do not care about us' (Source 8).

The conditions in the trenches were terrible. They were damp and dirty and full of rats and lice, and very cramped. The rats and lice spread diseases like typhus. The trenches were so full of water and mud that thousands of men got trench foot, when their feet went numb and then rotted away from infection. As this usually meant going to hospital or being sent home, the soldiers were quite pleased to get trench foot and some may have even got it deliberately (Source 4).

Morale sank very low towards the end of the War. George Morgan's description and the poem in Source 7 show that many soldiers became very disillusioned. They felt they did not have a chance and were bound to be killed. Some even mutinied against their officers, but anyone who mutinied, disobeyed an order or deserted was shot. The officers had to keep very strict discipline which meant that most men did as they were told.

An answer at Level 8

Notice that the Level 8 answer:

- questions the reliability of the evidence

- compares different interpretations of the same events

- includes original research and information given from the sources and key words above.

This is how to master the skill of historical enquiry.

Trench warfare developed in the First World War due to the failure of the German Schlieffen plan to end the war before Christmas 1914. The Russians had mobilised more quickly than expected and the British had sent over their small army to Belgium sooner than expected. The allies held the line at the Battle of the Marne, and so the Germans dug into deep trenches on high ground, along a line from the Belgian coast to the Swiss border. The allies built their own trenches and then sat facing the Germans over an area that came to be known as no-man's-land. This set the scene for trench warfare. The advantage was always with the defender of a trench in this situation, so attacks cost a lot of lives and were usually unsuccessful. Given the terrible conditions that existed in the trenches and the awful casualties involved, it is hardly surprising that disillusionment set in after a while and the officers had to enforce strict discipline to get things done.

The trenches were dug in zigzag lines to make them difficult to capture and hold. Parapets made of sandbags were placed at the top of the trench, with machine guns and periscopes, so that men could look out into no-man's-land. Rolls of barbed wire were placed in front of the trench to slow down any attack. All this made it very hard to attack a trench, and even if the enemy did get into a trench, they were difficult to hold. Large groups of infantry, armed only with rifles, bayonets and grenades, would charge at the enemy over no-man's-land. Since it was easy to shoot down rows of attacking infantry at a time, the losses were huge. Men felt like they were being sent to their deaths because they did not seem to have a fair chance of defending themselves. Men like George Morgan in Source 8 became bitter and disillusioned as a result, suggesting that the Commanders were engaged in a war of attrition where the loss of life did not seem to matter. The British Commander, Douglas Haig said the allies would win the war simply because they had more men than the Germans. If the losses were equal on both sides, the allies would be left with more men at the end!

No, sir, I can't see where we're going... only where we've been for the last 3 years!

However, there is a view that the Commanders did not have much alternative to these attacks, since no new, effective weapons existed. Several weapons were tried without success. One common tactic was to build bigger guns to shell the enemy prior to an attack. The shelling by the British before the Battle of the Somme was so great it was heard in Britain. Yet it warned the enemy and churned up the ground, making an attack more difficult. Gas was also used but if the wind was blowing in the wrong direction it could harm your own side! Aeroplanes were too flimsy to fly long distances or carry many bombs or men, so they were mainly used for reconnaissance. Tanks were invented in 1916, but were not effective until the Battle of Cambrai in 1917. Also there were factors beyond the Commander's control, like the shortage of shells for the British army in 1915-16. So the Commanders may not have been entirely to blame for the huge loss of life.

Conditions in the trenches were appalling. They were so thick with mud that soldiers had to walk on duck boards to avoid sinking and they were so dirty that rats and lice were commonplace. The rats even attacked men and could cause serious injury. Food was basic and diseases like trench fever and typhus spread quickly. Thousands suffered from trench foot, a rotting of the foot caused by standing in mud for long periods of time. For others, the experience led to psychological problems like shell shock. The soldiers who lived in these conditions became weary and desperate to go home (Source 7). Yet the commanders responded by enforcing very strict discipline on the men, anyone who deserted or mutinied was executed. Some men began to question the whole point of the war, believing that it was a war for the rich fought by the poor. However, the number of British soldiers who mutinied was remarkably small considering the awful conditions and horrific losses.

It is no wonder that to the generation of men who fought the war it was always called the 'Great War'. It was meant to be the war that ended all wars. These men would never be the same again.

Additional questions

Continue to further your skills of historical enquiry by attempting the following questions. Some concepts are included for you to consider:

 1 The causes of the First World War

Do you think the First World War was inevitable?

Alliance systems	An agreement between countries. Before the First World War, two major alliances existed: the Triple Alliance (1882) between Germany, Austria-Hungary and Italy and the Triple Entente (1907) between Britain, France and Russia.
Kaiser Wilhelm II	King of Germany at the outbreak of war. He had built up Germany's navy and sought a huge empire (like that of England and France).
Self-determination	Within Europe there were many nationalities living in different Empires (eg Austria-Hungarian Empire) who were discontented. They wished to be free of foreign rule.
Rivalries	European countries, eg Britain and Germany became rivals or competitors. Countries wanted to achieve success in overseas trade and the building of empires.
Naval race	Before 1914, Britain and Germany were involved in a 'race' to dominate the sea. In 1906, Britain developed the *Dreadnought*, the most advanced battleship ever built. Germany responded by building more battleships. The 'race' gathered speed.

2 The First World War at home

How did the First World War affect civilians at home?

War at sea

The first clash of British and German battleships happened at the Battle of Jutland in May 1916. The Germans tried to beat the British navy by developing the U-boat or submarine, which was designed to stop British trade and the import of food and supplies (leading to rationing). The bombing of the British liner, the *Lusitania*, in May 1915 by a German submarine caused controversy and outcry.

Conscription

Introduced to Britain in 1916 to ensure there were enough soldiers trained for the war. At the onset of war, many men had volunteered for the army. They were patriotic and wanted to fight for their country. This attitude changed when the war continued and thousands of men were losing their lives.

War at home

This refers to the experience of civilians, ordinary people living in Britain during the war. Britain, as an island, felt quite secure until the Germans began bombing with zeppelins. Zeppelins were large airships and were sent on night raids to destroy British military targets. During the war, 564 civilians were killed and 1370 injured. Civilians also suffered because although rationing ensured everyone had food, the amounts allowed were often small.

3 The Treaty of Versailles

Was the Treaty of Versailles a successful solution to the problems at the end of the First World War?

Treaty of Versailles	A conference was held to ensure peace after the Armistice on 11 November 1918. Held at Versailles in 1919, it was attended by the leaders of the victorious countries, but dominated by the ideas of Woodrow Wilson (the USA President) and his Fourteen Points. Germany was not allowed to attend, but had to agree to the recommendations of the conference, including the paying of reparations and the signing of the war-guilt clause. This was to cause severe discontent within Germany.
League of Nations	An idea of Woodrow Wilson in 1919, which was designed to help maintain peace and solve disputes by discussion rather than war.
Self-determination	The Treaty of Versailles created discontent because some ethnic minorities were ruled by another country. For example, the Sudeten Germans wanted self-determination and freedom from Czech rule. Hitler exploited this discontent in September 1939.

4 The Second World War – 1

How important was the conflict between political ideas in the build up to the Second World War?

Adolf Hitler	Born in 1889 in Austria. By 1921, Hitler was leader of the National Socialist German Workers' Party, commonly known as the Nazi Party. He sought to win back Germany's supremacy and to rebuild their military strength after the humiliation of the Treaty of Versailles. His party believed that the Aryan race should be dominant.
Dictatorship	A political system where one leader rules supreme.
Democracy	A political system where the people choose their own leaders through elections. Britain and the USA are democracies.
Communism	A belief that all people should be equal, ie that the class system should be abolished. Communists believe that this can only be achieved by revolution. For example, Lenin was dictator of Russia and a Communist.
Fascism	A one-party state which controls the lives of ordinary people. Fascism has a violent and militaristic image. Fascists believe in a dictatorship, where everyone follows the leader and works to strengthen their country. They also hate Communists and in Germany they hated Jews as well. The Nazis were Fascists.
Socialism	A policy that wants to achieve equality for all, and state ownership of industry, but by systematic and peaceful methods.

5   The Second World War – 2

How was the Second World War different from any previous war?

Policy of appeasement	Britain and France followed this policy in the 1930s when dealing with Hitler and Mussolini (dictator of Italy). Negotiation and discussion were used to solve problems by talking rather than fighting. This policy is particularly associated with Chamberlain, Prime Minister of Britain 1937-40.
Allies	Britain, France and the USA.
Axis Powers	Germany, Italy and Japan.
Propaganda	The art of presenting information to influence the way people think. Propaganda techniques were particularly used by Hitler and Mussolini to ensure they had support for their policies and for their position as dictators.
Home Front	The experiences of people in Britain during the war. British civilians were particularly at risk during the Battle of Britain and the Blitz between 1940-41. The bombing of British cities killed 40,000 and made two million homeless. Families sought protection in air-raid shelters and many children were evacuated to safer places in the countryside.
Holocaust	The policy followed by Hitler towards the Jewish population. Hitler believed that the final solution to the Jewish problem lay in the mass slaughter of the whole Jewish population of Europe. This led to the existence of concentration camps such as Auschwitz.

Timeline 1914-1918

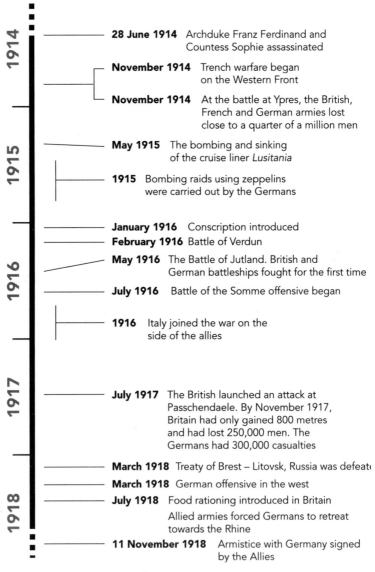

1914

28 June 1914 Archduke Franz Ferdinand and Countess Sophie assassinated

November 1914 Trench warfare began on the Western Front

November 1914 At the battle at Ypres, the British, French and German armies lost close to a quarter of a million men

1915

May 1915 The bombing and sinking of the cruise liner *Lusitania*

1915 Bombing raids using zeppelins were carried out by the Germans

1916

January 1916 Conscription introduced

February 1916 Battle of Verdun

May 1916 The Battle of Jutland. British and German battleships fought for the first time

July 1916 Battle of the Somme offensive began

1916 Italy joined the war on the side of the allies

1917

July 1917 The British launched an attack at Passchendaele. By November 1917, Britain had only gained 800 metres and had lost 250,000 men. The Germans had 300,000 casualties

1918

March 1918 Treaty of Brest – Litovsk, Russia was defeat

March 1918 German offensive in the west

July 1918 Food rationing introduced in Britain

Allied armies forced Germans to retreat towards the Rhine

11 November 1918 Armistice with Germany signed by the Allies

Timeline 1910-1950

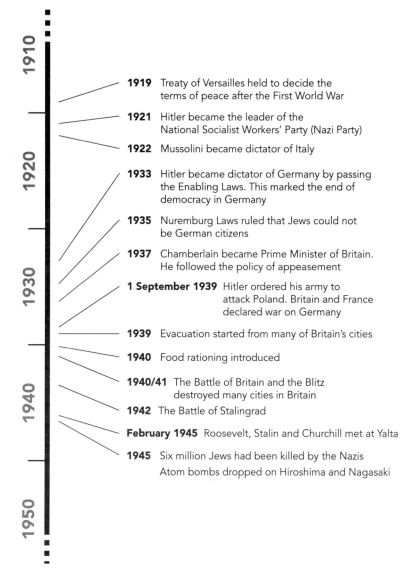

1910

1919 Treaty of Versailles held to decide the terms of peace after the First World War

1921 Hitler became the leader of the National Socialist Workers' Party (Nazi Party)

1922 Mussolini became dictator of Italy

1920

1933 Hitler became dictator of Germany by passing the Enabling Laws. This marked the end of democracy in Germany

1935 Nuremburg Laws ruled that Jews could not be German citizens

1937 Chamberlain became Prime Minister of Britain. He followed the policy of appeasement

1930

1 September 1939 Hitler ordered his army to attack Poland. Britain and France declared war on Germany

1939 Evacuation started from many of Britain's cities

1940 Food rationing introduced

1940/41 The Battle of Britain and the Blitz destroyed many cities in Britain

1940

1942 The Battle of Stalingrad

February 1945 Roosevelt, Stalin and Churchill met at Yalta

1945 Six million Jews had been killed by the Nazis Atom bombs dropped on Hiroshima and Nagasaki

1950

5 Organisation and communication

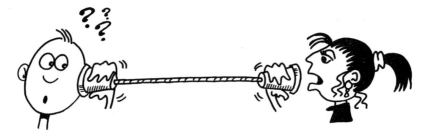

I said, 'Organisation'!

This chapter shows you how to combine the historical skills you have learned:

- *Chronology – Use time to place events and changes in order*

- *Knowledge and understanding – Give reasons and causes for events and changes*

- *Interpretations of history – Understand that different points of view lead to a variety of opinions and arguments*

- *Historical enquiry – Search sources and evidence to find out what really happened*

With expertise in these areas, you can organise and communicate your understanding of historical information drawn from a variety of sources. To organise and communicate effectively you:

- recall and select historical information, including dates and terms *(Level 1)*

- select, organise and deploy the terms necessary to describe and explain periods and topics *(Level 2)*

- select and organise historical information to produce structured work, including the appropriate use of dates and terms *(Level 3)*

- reach substantiated conclusions independently *(Level 4)*

- produce well structured narratives, descriptions and explanations, making appropriate use of dates and terms *(Level 5)*

- use a range of techniques including extended, structured writing; edit with a word processor; present data with charts and tables; make oral presentations to an audience; participate in an historical drama. *(Level 6)*

Level 3

At Level 3, you demonstrate factual knowledge of the main events, people and changes in the topic or period studied.

Use your textbook, notes and other references to answer the following questions:

1 What was the **date** (day, month, year) of the Bolshevik Revolution in Russia?

2 What was **Communism**?

3 Who was the **leader** of the Bolsheviks?

4 What was the **Cheka**?

5 Who were the **Reds** and **Whites** during the civil war?

6 With which country did Russia sign the **Treaty of Rapallo**?

4-6 Levels 4 to 6

You select and organise the evidence to produce structured work making use of dates and terms.

Study the headings below and use them to write an extended narrative which explains how German foreign policy between 1933-1939 helped bring about the outbreak of war in September 1939:

- Rearmament 1933-35
- Greater Reich
- Lebensraum
- Remilitarisation of the Rhineland
- Anschluss
- Munich Agreement
- Nazi-Soviet Pact

7+ Levels 7, 8 and GCSE grades A* to C

At higher levels you reach substantiated conclusions independently. You write well structured narratives, descriptions and explanations, making appropriate use of dates and terms.

Practice question

Hitler's rise to power

Using the sources and your own knowledge, identify how the Nazis won power between 1918 and 1933.

Study the information below and write an extended narrative which explains how Adolf Hitler and the Nazis won power in Germany between 1918 and 1933. Use these headings:

- The Versailles Treaty
- The origins of the Nazi Party
- Hitler's ideas for Germany
- Inflation and the Munich Putsch
- Gustav Stresemann and the Dawes Plan
- The Wall Street Crash
- Unemployment and Nazi Success

SOURCE 1 Adolf Hitler served as a corporal in the trenches during the First World War. He believed that the German army was not defeated in November 1918 but 'stabbed in the back' by politicians at home.

SOURCE 2 Hitler joined the German Workers' Party, which became the National Socialist German Workers' Party (NSDAP) or Nazis under his leadership. The Party blamed the Versailles Treaty and the Jews for all Germany's problems. Sturmabteilung (the SA or stormtroops) acted as bouncers at Nazi meetings and fought with rivals.

SOURCE 3 Hitler and the Nazis tried to seize power by armed force in Munich in 1923. Hitler was imprisoned when the Beer Hall Putsch failed. Hitler received national publicity for the first time and realised that he would have to win elections if he was serious about gaining power.

SOURCE 4 Hitler made little progress between 1924 and 1929. Gustav Stresemann ended inflation; wages improved; and under the Dawes Plan, American banks loaned Germany the money to pay off reparations.

SOURCE 5 The Wall Street Crash of 1929 caused mass unemployment in Germany as American banks called in their loans to cover losses on the stock market. In 1928, there was less than one million unemployed; by 1932 the figure had risen to six million. This created a serious crisis and the country looked for a strong man to solve the problem.

SOURCE 6 Under the terms of the Versailles Treaty, Germany accepted the blame for the war and agreed to pay compensation. Land occupied by German people was given to other countries created by the treaty.

SOURCE 7 In 1923, inflation caused the collapse of the German financial system and wiped out the savings of middle class people. The price of a loaf of bread rose from almost 1 mark in 1919 to over 200,000,000,000 marks by November 1923. Many Germans lost respect for the government and were more willing to support extremists like Hitler.

I'm just popping out for a loaf of bread

SOURCE 8 Hitler wrote *Mein Kampf (My Struggle)* while he was in prison. He outlined his main ideas:

- Germans were the master race
- Germans across Europe should be united as one people under one leader or Führer
- The Versailles Treaty should be torn up
- Jews and Communists should be destroyed
- Germans had the right to 'living room' or 'Lebensraum' in the east.

SOURCE 9 When the unemployment crisis came, Hitler was ready. He used:

- violent gangs to deal with opposition
- speeches at mass rallies to encourage emotion and enthusiasm
- propaganda to blame Jews and Communists
- promises to solve unemployment.

The Nazis won 12 seats in the Reichstag in 1928; 196 seats in 1932; and 233 seats in 1933.

Relevant concepts

The question on page 81 requires an understanding of the following concepts several of which you considered for your answer about political ideas in the Second World War (see page 74):

Anti-Communism   Hatred of Communists, Socialists and those with left-wing ideas.

Anti-Semitism   Hatred of Jews. Nazis believed the Jews were the enemies of Germany and blamed them for Communism, and all Germany's ills.

Democracy   (See page 74.)

Dictatorship   (See page 74.)

Fascism   (See page 74.)

Great Depression   The period from 1929-1935 was a time of immense hardship across the world. Prices were falling, businesses and banks were collapsing and unemployment was rising. This is called the Great Depression.

Greater Reich   The Nazis wanted all German speaking people to live inside Germany but many did not at that time. Some had their own separate country (Austria) while German minorities had been given to other countries by the peace treaties at the end of the war, eg the Sudentenland went to Czechoslovakia. Hitler wanted a Greater Reich to include all Germans, wherever they lived.

Lebensraum	Nazis also wanted an empire across Eastern Europe and Russia and for the people of those countries to become slaves to the Germans. This was called Lebensraum or living space.

I think you'll find the Lebensraum more than adequate...

Middle classes	In Germany these could be businessmen and women, professional people or even shopkeepers and office workers.
Nationalism	A strong belief in your country. The Nazis were violently nationalist, being prepared to start wars in order to increase Germany's power.
Propaganda	The art of presenting information to influence the way people think. Propaganda techniques were particularly used by Hitler and Mussolini to ensure they had support for their policies and for their positions as dictators.
Stab in the back myth	The myth that at the end of the First World War the German government gave up too soon and should have carried on the fighting. The German Chancellor (leader) during the First World War resigned shortly before the war ended and left a new leader (Ebert) and a new party (SDP) to sign the Armistice and so end the war with the allies. Nazis said Ebert and his supporters (including Jews and Communists) had stabbed Germany in the back by doing this.

Tackling the question

Before tackling the question on page 81 you should go through the following stages:

- read all the sources carefully
- make sure you understand the relevant concepts
- research the topic on your own
- select information that is appropriate for each heading
- plan out the structure of your answer
- look carefully at the level descriptions given at the start of this chapter.

Planning out the structure of an answer:

- The introduction should outline your overall conclusion. (Remember the rule: Conclude and then prove.)
- Each paragraph should start with a key sentence which sums up the key point of the paragraph.
- The rest of each paragraph should be devoted to proving the point made in the key sentence by using evidence.
- The last sentence of a paragraph should connect that paragraph to the paragraph that is to follow.
- The conclusion should outline your main argument and why you have reached that conclusion.

An answer at Level 5

Notice that this answer describes each point carefully and accurately. There are no factual mistakes. It starts with an argument in the introduction. Every paragraph makes a separate point and provides evidence to back it up, but:

- it shows little original research
- it does not establish the most important reasons for the rise of Hitler
- it does not consider different interpretations.

The Nazis came to power in 1933 because Germany was desperate for a new start with a strong and powerful leader who would restore prosperity and German pride.

The Treaty of Versailles was one reason. The treaty was signed by Germany in June 1919 and it forced Germany to accept blame for the war, the loss of a lot of her land, armed forces and industry, and a large bill (reparations) to pay for all the damage in the war. Some German-speaking people were transferred to other countries. All this made many Germans very angry. The politicians of the new Germany after the First World War (called the Weimar Republic) seemed to accept these harsh terms.

The Nazi party was first called the German Workers' Party but soon became known as the National Socialist German Workers' Party or NSDAP. They blamed Germany's bad times on the Jews and Communists and promised a stronger Germany which would stand up for itself against other countries. The Nazis got a brilliant new leader in 1920, Adolf Hitler. He was an excellent speaker who could excite a crowd with his ideas and win a lot of popular support. They used violent 'stormtroops', the SA or Brownshirts, to attack their opponents.

Hitler had some very extreme ideas for Germany. He wanted to smash the Treaty of Versailles and make Germany great again. He had plans to unite all German-speaking people into a Greater Reich and later to create a German empire in Eastern Europe, or Lebensraum. He wanted to be an all-powerful dictator who would be obeyed by everyone – a system he said would make Germany strong. He was a fierce anti-Communist and anti-Semite and blamed them for everything that had gone wrong. He also promised to get everyone back to work by creating millions of jobs for the German people. He wrote all these ideas down in a book called *Mein Kampf*.

At this time, few people knew about Hitler and the Nazis. However, between 1919-23 Germany was very unstable. There had been several attempts to overthrow the government and the government made the mistake of printing extra money to try and get itself out of debt. This led to hyper-inflation which meant that prices were rising to ridiculously high levels. The price of a loaf of bread rose from almost one Mark in 1919 to over 200,000,000,000 Marks by November 1923. The middle classes found their savings were worthless and began to support the more extreme parties.

In November 1923, Hitler tried to take over the government. He linked up with Erich Ludendorff, a First World War general, and organised a march on the government offices in Munich from a Beer Hall in the city. It was a total failure and Hitler was imprisoned, although only for 9 months in a luxury cell. This is where he wrote *Mein Kampf*. Hitler now believed that the best way to power was firstly to win an election.

However, when Hitler got out of prison Germany was becoming more prosperous again. She had a new leader, Gustav Stresemann, who ended the inflation, and arranged a large loan from America known as the Dawes Plan (1924) which helped Germany pay back her reparations bill. Between 1924-29 prosperity improved so much that the German middle classes forgot about extremists like Hitler.

Unfortunately, all that changed in October 1929 when the Wall Street Crash in America started off the Great Depression. Unemployment rocketed to six million and poverty was widespread. Once again businesses and banks collapsed but this time prices and wages fell. The working classes turned to Communism and Socialism for support. This frightened the middle classes who feared their property was going to be taken away from them.

Hitler and the Nazis promised to stop the Communists and Socialists. They promised to cure unemployment and poverty and make Germany great again. They used posters, marches and speeches as propaganda to get their point across. Hitler was a powerful figure. The German middle classes turned to him to save them from disaster. In 1928, the Nazis had only 12 seats in the parliament or Reichstag but by 1932 they had 196. The SA threatened Jews and Communists and so made it difficult for Hitler's enemies to fight back. All this ended up persuading the German President, Hindenberg, to appoint Hitler as Chancellor in January 1933. Once in power, Hitler never looked back.

An answer at Level 8

This answer introduces lots of outside research. It starts by explaining what is considered to be the most important reason for the rise to power of the Nazis. It examines a wide range of interpretations as to why the Nazis rose to power, and reaches careful conclusions through a detailed examination of the evidence. These are all features of an excellent answer.

> Hitler and the Nazis won power in Germany primarily because the country had not fully recovered from the effects of the First World War when it was further affected by the Great Depression sweeping in from the USA in late 1929. This gave the appearance that German society was collapsing which in turn encouraged the middle classes to turn to Fascism to save them from the threat of Communism. Hitler was able to exploit this situation to his advantage.
>
> The seeds of the Second World War were probably sown in 1919 when Germany was forced to sign the Treaty of Versailles. This was a humiliation and an economic and political disaster since it forced the Germans to accept total blame for starting the war, and took land, resources, money and a large part of their armed forces away from them. It meant that German nationalism was embittered and Germany faced an uncertain economic future. It also meant that millions of German-speaking people were placed outside Germany, creating a potentially serious problem for the countries where they now lived – at some point Germany might want them back.
>
> These points help explain the rise of the Nazis because the party first appeared as the German Workers' Party in 1920, shortly after the treaty was signed. It was quickly taken over by Adolf Hitler, whose brilliant ability to speak to crowds was a decisive factor both then and in the 1930s. At this time, the party was a mixture of left wing and right wing ideas, although later it was to drop most of its left wing ideas so as not to upset too many of the Nazis' big business supporters.
>
> Hitler's message was not yet widely known. The Nazis were a small party although they became better known as Hitler himself started to promote his ideas. Even then, in the early 1920s the conditions were not right to get the Nazis too much support. The Weimar republic was still quite new and the German middle classes were willing to back democracy at least for the time being. However, the development of hyper-inflation from 1920 onwards eroded their confidence. The price of a loaf of bread rose from almost one Mark in 1919 to an amazing 200,000,000,000 Marks by November 1923. Anyone who had savings, and most of the middle class did, found that they disappeared

almost overnight. Businesses collapsed and, had the situation continued, it is highly likely that the middle classes would have turned to the more extreme parties for help. As it happened, Hitler and the Nazis did try and take over in Munich, with the help of General Ludendorff in the famous Beer Hall Putsch. The people were not ready however, and the middle classes were not happy to support a violent uprising. The Putsch was a fiasco and the army stayed loyal to the government. However, there is proof that people did have some sympathy for Hitler's message by the way the judge at his trial gave him such a light sentence and the press reports spoke about Hitler's strong character.

All this is evidence that something else needed to happen before the Nazis could hope to take power. They had some support, but not enough. In jail Hitler outlined his Fascist ideas in more depth. He wrote of how he wanted to make Germany great again and how she had been stabbed in the back by the Jews and Communists. He said they had organised Germany's downfall in the First World War and her humiliation over the Versailles Treaty. He was a violent anti-Semite and anti-Communist and blamed them for all Germany's problems. He planned to sweep away the Versailles Treaty and replace it with a Greater Reich of German-speaking people and eventually Lebensraum or living space for the German people in a huge empire in Eastern Europe and Russia. This would almost certainly mean war. He also had plans to restore the German economy to prosperity and return Germany to a mythical past when men and women followed traditional roles and everyone was loyal to their community. Of course, he hated democracy. All this was published in his book *Mein Kampf.*

We should notice that when Hitler came out of jail in 1925, support for the Nazis had fallen sharply. In 1923, Gustav Stresemann had led Germany successfully out of the period of hyper-inflation and as foreign minister in 1924 had negotiated the Dawes Plan with the USA, Britain and France which allowed Germany to suspend her reparations payments for two years and gave her a large American loan to help pay off her debts. By 1925, the world economy was picking up and prosperity was starting to return. The middle classes were more secure and less likely to go for anything extreme. Hitler's chance seemed to have gone.

The chance returned in 1929. Just as Germany was finding its feet, the Wall Street Crash in America sent the world economy into chaos. The bank loans given to Germany under the Dawes Plan were recalled and banks and businesses collapsed everywhere. Prices, wages and output fell and world trade slumped. This was disaster for Germany. Unemployment rose to six million by 1932 from less than one million in 1928. Support for the Communist party grew amongst the working classes and this caused panic amongst the middle classes who feared losing their property. Support for the democratic parties faded and instead middle-class support for the Nazis grew. Now the Nazi message made more sense. Their ideas about smashing Communism attracted the support of big businesses and blaming the Jews was an easy way for people to find a scapegoat. The less aggressive policies of the democratic parties seemed to have failed.

By 1932, the Nazis had become the largest party in Germany with 196 seats in the Reichstag or German Parliament. By January 1933, Hitler had been appointed Chancellor by the elderly President Paul Von Hindenberg and by March the Nazis had won a great election victory getting 233 seats. The election result was overshadowed by the fire which destroyed the Reichstag. The Nazis used this incident to pin the blame on the Communists and arrest many of their leaders.

The Nazis would not therefore have come to power without the Great Depression. The Treaty of Versailles, the popularity of Hitler and his ideas and the economic problems of the early 1920s were all contributory factors but, undoubtedly, it was the effects of the Depression, coming when Germany was just starting to recover her strength, that was the main reason for the rise to power of the Nazis.

Additional questions

Good organisation and communication is vital for examination success. Consider the following questions to develop your expertise in this area of historical analysis and to assist your ability to extract relevant information.

 1 Lenin comes to power: October 1917

What were Lenin's views when he took control of Russia?

This question is designed to test your knowledge of Lenin's thoughts and opinions about Russia when he took power in 1917.

Imagine that you are Lenin. It is your first day in power (26 October 1917) and you are issuing a set of decrees or laws to the Russian people. As Lenin, you must write a speech detailing your ideas relating to 'peace, land, bread and freedom'.

You must include the following:

- your ideas about the nationalisation of land
- your ideas about the abolition of social classes
- your ideas about Russia's involvement in the First World War.

Remember to write as if you are Lenin. In what style did he speak and write? Study existing speeches to help you.

2 Stalin in power: Economic policies

How important was the Stakhanovite Movement in 1935?

Stalin established Five Year Plans to increase industrial production and economic success in Russia. The success of his economic policies has been the subject of many historical debates. However, there is little doubt that Stalin was a master at using propaganda to achieve his goals.

Study Stalin's economic policies and identify information relating to the Stakhanovite movement. Try to answer the following questions:

- What was the Stakhanovite movement?
- How did it get its name?
- When, why and how did it begin?
- How and why did Stalin encourage the methods of the Stakhanovite movement in 1935?

Once you have selected the relevant information, try the following task, which will test your ability to organise your thoughts and ideas.

It is October 1935 and you are a supporter of Stalin's Five Year Plans. You desperately want to help your country succeed. You work in a large factory manufacturing tractors and farming machinery. Write a diary entry explaining your feelings about your work, Stalin and the Stakhanovite movement.

3 Roosevelt and the New Deal

How did the New Deal affect American society?

In 1932, Roosevelt was faced with the difficult task of solving America's deep economic depression. His answer was the New Deal.

Using your knowledge of this period, either in a group or individually, write two short pieces of drama/play script showing the impact of the New Deal on groups of people in American society. Choose between (a) a farmer, (b) an industrial worker, (c) a young unemployed person or (d) a trade union representative.

Your characters could:

- show their feelings towards Hoover and Roosevelt
- explain their problems to friends or family
- show their everyday circumstances and the changes which Roosevelt makes.

The economy was depressed and, try as he might, Franklin could not cheer it up...

4 Hitler plans for war: 1937

Was Germany ready for war in 1937?

In 1937, Hitler held a secret meeting with his advisors and army commanders. At this meeting Hitler informed them of his intentions for war.

Imagine you are one of Hitler's assistants. Your task is to prepare a report regarding Germany's potential for undertaking and winning a war on a world scale. Hitler has demanded the following information:

- Statistics and conclusions relating to (a) economic strength and (b) military strength
- The extent of support and opposition to his policies
- Details about Germany's readiness for war.

You must prepare this information for a report, including data in the form of charts and tables. This task will help you to develop your ICT skills. Remember to edit your first draft to ensure your report is concise and readable.

Timeline 1900-1945

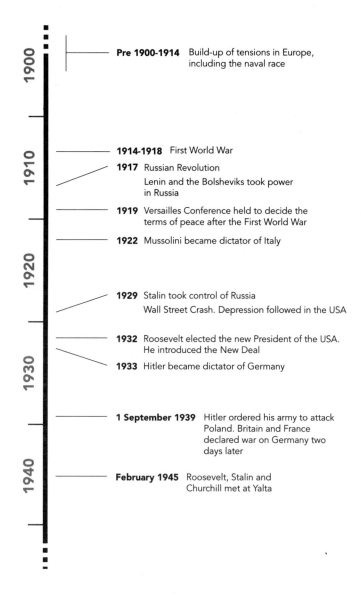

1900

Pre 1900-1914 Build-up of tensions in Europe, including the naval race

1910

1914-1918 First World War

1917 Russian Revolution
Lenin and the Bolsheviks took power in Russia

1919 Versailles Conference held to decide the terms of peace after the First World War

1922 Mussolini became dictator of Italy

1920

1929 Stalin took control of Russia
Wall Street Crash. Depression followed in the USA

1932 Roosevelt elected the new President of the USA. He introduced the New Deal

1933 Hitler became dictator of Germany

1930

1 September 1939 Hitler ordered his army to attack Poland. Britain and France declared war on Germany two days later

1940

February 1945 Roosevelt, Stalin and Churchill met at Yalta

6 Sourcework skills at GCSE

To be successful at GCSE History you must have good sourcework skills. Learn and follow the simple rules outlined in this chapter and most of the battle is won.

All students between the ages of 11-14 study the topics that we have covered so far in this book. Unfortunately, not all GCSE courses have the same content so it is not possible to look at all the topics that could be studied at GCSE within this final chapter. The good news is that whatever GCSE course you follow, the skills required are always the same. Therefore, this chapter applies equally to everyone who wants to succeed at GCSE.

The sources in this chapter are based on the topics that have been covered in earlier chapters. This is so that everyone is familiar with them. The skills can be applied to any topic you are studying. You should check with your teacher, however, to ensure that you know which exam papers test sourcework skills most, as this may vary from course to course.

Sourcework skills

To have good sourcework skills you will need to be able to:

- comprehend sources and make inferences from them
- comprehend sources by using your own knowledge and making inferences from them
- assess the reliability of sources for use in a particular historical enquiry, using your own knowledge
- assess whether the information provided in a source is sufficient to answer a particular historical enquiry
- evaluate the usefulness of a source for a particular historical enquiry
- explain why two interpretations of the same event differ
- assess the reliability of interpretations.

Comprehending a source and making inferences

Sourcework questions require you to comprehend a source. This means, quite simply, that you have to understand it. Sources have to be understood before they can be used. Next, you have to infer something from a source. This means to work out the implications of what is said. Most questions that test your comprehension of a source also test your ability to draw inferences from it.

Look at the following source. It is a plan of a trench from the First World War (see Chapter 4):

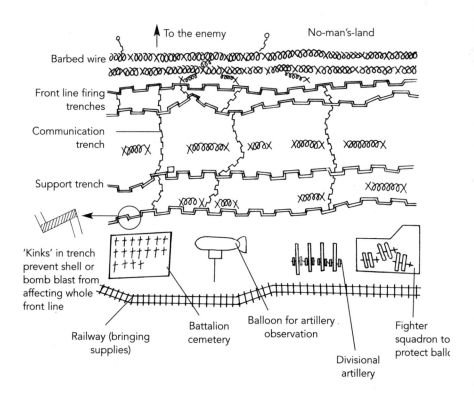

What does this source tell us about the nature of trench warfare in the First World War?

A good answer here would:

- recognise that the plan shows a very well defended position

- conclude that attacks against such positions would be very hard to make and that therefore the defenders of trenches had a great advantage.

Questions like this require you to use your own knowledge in the answer. In this case you could add that:

- attackers were usually infantry, armed only with rifles and bayonets, or perhaps grenades. This was little use against the machine guns and barbed wire of the enemy

- most attacks were preceded by an artillery barrage. The shells were meant to destroy the enemy trenches but generally they only had the effect of churning up no-man's-land, making it difficult to cross.

You could conclude that the nature of trench warfare led to huge casualties and little gain. Hence the war reached a stalemate position.

The key is to recognise that you need to draw conclusions from the source which are not directly shown within it.

Sufficiency of evidence

It is common to ask if there is sufficient (enough) evidence in a source to answer a particular historical question.

For example, read the following source about the Peterloo Massacre (see Chapter 3):

> **SOURCE** A letter to the *Courier*, expressing an eyewitness view of the Peterloo massacre of 1819
>
> *The meeting was then addressed by the several orators, showing much menacing attitude, and the shouts seemed to rend the very air and shake the foundation of the ground. The constables were tauntingly insulted wherever they were observed to stand.*
>
> *Consequently, the cavalry charged in their own defence; not without first being witness to a pistol shot from the multitude, against one of the gentlemen in our yeomanry, who now lies in imminent danger.*

Does this source provide sufficient information to prove that the Manchester magistrates were justified in ordering the cavalry to charge on the crowd at St Peter's Field in 1819?

Your approach would need to do two things:

1   Outline the information that the source provides which does help to justify this action (eg the crowd were provoking the cavalry).

2   Provide other factual points, not given in the source, which shed further light on the question (eg that the Prime Minister, Lord Liverpool, privately expressed the view that the magistrates had been rather hasty in sending in the cavalry).

For these sorts of questions you must always conclude that the source is useful up to a point.

Never say:

- the source is useless, or alternatively that it contains everything you need to know

- the source has some value but that it would be nice to have more eyewitness accounts, views of people involved, statistics (without ever actually giving any specific factual evidence).

You have to introduce facts from your own knowledge to shed more light on the information given by the source.

Reliability of sources

It is essential to be able to assess the reliability of a source for GCSE. There are two stages to this process:

- compare the facts and opinions given in the source with other facts and opinions you are aware of from your own knowledge. If they back each other up then the source is likely to be reliable; if not then the reverse is true. In fact, a source is usually somewhere in between these two extremes

- examine the source itself for signs of bias, exaggeration and distortion; whether it is deliberate or otherwise. The more evidence of this you find, the more unreliable the source.

After these two stages you will have established how reliable the source is. To conclude, it is a good idea to use the information given about the source to explain its reliability.

For example, read the following source about the First World War (see Chapter 4):

SOURCE Field Marshall Haig writing in 1917 about the battle of the Somme which had taken place in the previous year

By the third week in November, the three main objects with which we had commenced our offensive had been achieved. Verdun had been relieved; the main German forces had been held on the Western Front; and the enemy's strength had been very considerably worn down.

How reliable is this account of the Battle of the Somme?

To answer this question you would need to:

1   Compare Haig's account with facts you already know about the battle. In this case, it is what Haig leaves out of his account which makes the source unreliable. He fails to refer to the huge British losses and the small amount of land gained. These are very important to any historian wishing to assess the success of the battle. On the other hand, the original aim of the attack was to take the pressure off the French troops further south at Verdun, and German troops were in fact forced away from that battle and towards the Somme.

2   Examine the way in which the source was written. It uses very positive phrases like 'already.....achieved' and 'enemy's strength.........worn down.' Haig makes it sound like the battle was an unquestionable success.

3   Explain that Haig was writing in wartime, a year after the battle, as the man who was most responsible for the attack at the Somme. He had his own reputation and the morale of the country to consider. To admit that the battle was a failure would be to invite criticism of his leadership and risk lowering the morale of the country.

From this you could deduce that Haig's account was at best only partially reliable. He did not tell any actual lies but he left out key pieces of evidence about the battle, and had every incentive to do so.

Usefulness of sources

Often at GCSE there are questions which ask how useful a source is to a particular historical enquiry. This involves two stages:

1   Assessing the reliability of the source. The more reliable the source is, the more useful it is, although even very unreliable sources are still useful.

2   Making inferences (conclusions) from the source.

For example, read the following source about the dissolution of the English monasteries (see Chapter 2):

> **SOURCE** Report given to Thomas Cromwell by one of the inspectors whom he chose to investigate the state of the English monasteries in 1535
>
> *The Abbot (of St Edmund's monastery in Suffolk) delighted much in playing at dice and in that spent much money. For his own pleasure he has had lots of beautiful buildings built.*

To tackle this consider how useful this source would be to an historian investigating the reasons why King Henry VIII dissolved the English monasteries in 1536.

This account suggests that the monks were a worthless lot who were more interested in their own pleasure than in serving God or the wider community. Now find other factual evidence. Does it back up the source or reveal a different picture?

If the source is reliable, it shows that King Henry had good reason to dissolve the monasteries. If the source is only partially true then it is still useful because it shows us that Cromwell wanted to find evidence that the monks were idle and selfish so that he could give King Henry an excuse to dissolve the monasteries.

Examining interpretations

At GCSE, you are required to compare different interpretations of the same events. You may be asked to explain why the interpretations are different.

You could start by finding out two things about the authors of each of the interpretations:

1 Were they in a position to know all the evidence? For example, did they only know some of the facts of the case?

2 Did their position, the time they were writing, or who they were writing for, give them an incentive to lie or at least deliberately distort the truth?

You might be asked to explain which of the interpretations is most accurate. If so, assess the reliability of both interpretations in the manner described earlier.

For example, read the following two interpretations. Both are concerned with the rise to power of the Nazis in Germany (see Chapter 5).

SOURCE In February 1933, the German parliament or Reichstag burnt down only a few days before a national election was to be held. The Nazis blamed their greatest rivals the Communists for this act of violence and had many Communists arrested and imprisoned. As a result, the Nazis did very well in the subsequent elections.

Communist International Propaganda Organisation, 1933

SOURCE In view of the ever growing anti-Fascist (anti-Nazi) feeling amongst the workers, Hitler's election prospects were not good. It became necessary to change the situation by some act of provocation. Then the elections could be carried out when violent feeling against the Communists and the Socialists was at its height.

W Laquer, Historian, 1971

Latest evidence tends to acquit the Nazis of this particular crime.

Why do these two interpretations differ? Which is the more accurate of these interpretations? You should consider the following points:

Clearly, the Communists had a good incentive as they were wrongly accused by the Nazis. The historian, on the other hand, was writing well after the Nazis had fallen from power and was not going to be directly affected by the outcome of the fire.

To answer the second question, explain that there was a half crazed Dutchman, Marinus Van der Lubbe, who was found at the scene of the fire carrying firelighting equipment and Communist party documents. On the other hand, one eyewitness to the fire said he saw Hitler look at the fire and then say immediately 'We'll show them' and 'Every Communist official must be shot', which suggests that the Nazis made up the accusations against the Communists without actually knowing whether they started the fire or not. Your conclusion could be that the historian was right to say that there is no evidence to say the Nazis did start the fire but the Communist was right in saying that the Nazis were keen to take advantage of the situation regardless of who was really to blame for starting it.

Practice question

Causes of the Second World War

1 Rearmament

Examine Source 1:

SOURCE 1 numbers of aircraft built by France, Britain and Germany, 1933-39

	1933	1935	1937	1939
France	600	785	743	3163
Britain	633	1140	2123	7940
Germany	368	3183	5606	8295

Using Source 1, and your own knowledge, explain why Britain and France began to follow a policy of appeasement after 1934.

Tackling the question

To answer this question, firstly explain that the rapid production of aircraft by Germany between 1933-39 would put Britain and France in a weak military position if war broke out. This encouraged Chamberlain to seek a peaceful solution to German demands.

In addition, you could show your knowledge of:

- The threat of war posed by German foreign policy. Give examples such as the Anschluss (March 1938) or the Sudetenland crisis (September 1938).

- The terrible consequences of the First World War. With new weapons like the long range bomber plane another war promised to be even worse. German dive bombers had been used to cause havoc in the Spanish Civil War. Such a war frightened public opinion in Britain and France, which in turn put pressure on their governments to follow a policy of appeasement.

- The argument that Germany had been harshly treated in the Treaty of Versailles. This was shown by the British economist J M Keynes who argued that Germany could not afford the huge reparations bill imposed on her by the treaty. By the 1930s, there was a feeling that Germany deserved to be treated more fairly and that standing up to her aggressively was not the right approach.

2 Hitler's Foreign Policy

Examine Source 2:

SOURCE 2 Adolf Hitler's Political Testament, 1945

It is untrue that I or anyone else in Germany wanted war in 1939.

How reliable is Source 2 as an indicator of Hitler's foreign policy aims in the period 1937-39? Use your own knowledge to help your answer.

Tackling the question

You must start by using your own knowledge to assess the reliability of the source:

- The details of the Four Year Plan, 1936-40 (ie rearmament, autarky). Germany was building an economy fit to fight a war.

- German foreign policy aims included creating Lebensraum (an empire across eastern Europe and the Soviet Union). This was bound to lead to clashes with countries like Poland and the Soviet Union.

- The Nazi-Soviet pact between Germany and the Soviet Union said that neither country would attack the other. Hitler's motive was to ensure that he could attack Poland without facing war with the Soviet Union.

All these points suggest that the statement made by Hitler in Source 2 is unreliable.

Finally, you could explain that the date of the source (1945, when Germany was on the brink of defeat) indicates that Hitler was trying to avoid taking responsibility for a war that had turned into a complete disaster for Germany.

3 The Nazi-Soviet Pact

Examine Source 3:

SOURCE 3 Article 1 of the Nazi-Soviet Pact, 23 August 1939

> Both parties obligate themselves to desist from any act of violence, any aggressive action, and any attack on each other, either individually or jointly with other powers.

How useful would Source 3 be in helping the historian to explain why war broke out in September 1939?

Tackling the question

You should use your own knowledge to assess whether the source is reliable. Any extra facts about the Nazi-Soviet pact would prove whether it is reliable or not. For example:

- A very good example would be to say that the source only shows the part of the pact that was made public. Another, secret agreement was made to partition Poland following an attack on her by Germany and the Soviet Union.

Now you should use your own knowledge to explain how this pact would be useful to an historian studying the reasons for the outbreak of the war:

- It shows that this pact opened the way for Germany to invade Poland. Hitler knew this might start a war with Britain and France, since both of them had given a guarantee to defend Poland. However, Hitler wanted to avoid war with the Soviet Union at the same time so signed the Nazi-Soviet pact.

Finally, you should explain some other reasons for the outbreak of war which are not covered in the source. These are mainly long term reasons for the outbreak of the war. This is to prove that the source is only useful to a certain extent.

For example:

- It does not explain that the policy of appeasement, followed by Britain and France up to 1939, had encouraged Hitler to keep increasing his demands until war became highly likely; such as by allowing the Anschluss to take place which then encouraged Hitler to demand the Sudetenland.

- It does not explain that part of the reason why Germany had developed such an aggressive foreign policy was that she had been humiliated by the Treaty of Versailles after the First World War.

Therefore the source only gives us the short term reason for the outbreak of war in 1939.

4 The Munich Agreement

Examine Sources 4 and 5:

SOURCE 4 Neville Chamberlain in a letter to his former Prime Minister and Conservative colleague, Stanley Baldwin, 17 October 1940

Never for one single instant have I doubted the rightness of what I did at Munich. My critics differed from me because they were ignorant. So I regret nothing in the past.

SOURCE 5 Winston Churchill, October 1938, House of Commons

The Munich Agreement is a total and unmitigated disaster.

a   Why do these two views of the Munich Agreement differ?

b   Which is the most reliable version of the results of the Munich Agreement?

To answer part a of the question you need to give reasons *why* (as opposed to how) the two interpretations differ.

Examples of good points could include the following:

- The Munich Agreement was a short term success for Chamberlain and Britain in that it avoided war in September 1938 when Britain's air defences were weak. When war did break out in September 1939 they were stronger.

- In the source Chamberlain says that he knew something at the time of the Munich Agreement that people outside the government, such as Churchill, would not have known. This was probably that Britain was likely to lose a war against Germany if one had begun at this time.

- In the source Chamberlain defends his own policy. After all, he had not been successful in preventing war breaking out, so he wanted to rescue his reputation.

- Churchill was probably thinking that by the time of the Munich Agreement Hitler had already shown that he was keen to expand by using force. For example, in the Anschluss of March 1938, Hitler had forced the Austrian Chancellor, Schuschnigg, to accept the Austrian Nazi Party into the government. To Churchill this was proof that a policy of appeasement was unlikely to work with Hitler.

- Churchill believed that appeasement would only encourage aggressive dictators like Hitler to make greater demands in the future, whereas Chamberlain believed that Hitler would be satisfied if he was allowed to get his way on issues like the Sudetenland.

Part b is really about assessing the reliability of both these interpretations by using your own knowledge.

Evidence that supports 4 and disagrees with 5:

- Britain had a lot fewer aircraft than Germany in September 1938 (see Source 1).

- War was avoided in September 1938 and the Munich Agreement was responsible for this.

111

- Britain was in a stronger position to fight Germany in September 1939.

Evidence that supports 5 and disagrees with 4:

- Hitler did not keep his promises in the Munich Agreement. Within six months he had ordered the invasion of Western Czechoslovakia.

- Hitler had shown that he had little regard for international agreements well before Munich. He had broken the Treaty of Versailles on a range of issues, starting in 1933 when he had cancelled Germany's reparation payments to Britain and France.

- War broke out in September 1939. Appeasement had failed in its main aim of avoiding war.

In conclusion, therefore, Chamberlain was right in that the Munich Agreement was in some senses a short term success, but in the long run Churchill's assessment was the more sensible.

Skills Progress Chart

You may like to keep a chart of your progress in history by using the following table. As you reach each skill level, fill in the date and sign your initials in the student confirmation box. Then ask your teacher to sign their initials in the teacher confirmation box.

History skills and Levels		Date achieved	Confirmation	
			Student	Teacher
Level	**Chronology**			
2	I can place familiar objects in chronological order and make distinctions between aspects of our own lives and past times			
3	I can show my understanding of chronology by my increasing awareness that the past can be divided into different periods of time. I can describe changes over a period of time			
4	I can describe the characteristic features of past societies and periods and can identify change and continuity within and across periods			
5	I can describe events and people. I can distinguish between different kinds of historical change			
	Knowledge and understanding			
2	I can suggest reasons why people in the past acted as they did and I can identify differences between past and present times			
3	I am beginning to give a few reasons for, and results of, historical events or developments and can identify differences between times in the past			
4	I can show awareness that historical events usually have more than one cause and consequence and can describe different features of an historical period			
5	I can describe and make links between relevant reasons for, and results of, events and changes			

6	I can examine, and am beginning to analyse the reasons for, and results of events and changes. I understand that causes and consequences can vary in importance and can describe past societies and periods and can make links between features within and across periods			
7	I can analyse reasons for, and results of, events and changes. I can show how different causes of an historical event are connected and can analyse relationships between features of a particular period or society. I can describe how different people's ideas and attitudes within that period or society are often related to their circumstances			
8	My expectations and analysis of, reasons for, and results of events and changes are set in their wider historical context and I can analyse the relationships between events, people and changes and between the features of past societies			
	Interpretations of history			
2	I can identify some of the different ways the past is represented			
3	I can identify some of the different ways in which the past is represented. I can distinguish between a fact and a point of view			
4	I can show an understanding that deficiencies in evidence may lead to different interpretations of the past and show how some aspects of the past have been represented and interpreted in different ways			
5	I understand that events, people and changes have been interpreted in different ways and I can suggest possible reasons for this			
6	I can describe, and am beginning to explain, different historical interpretations of events and changes. I can demonstrate how historical interpretations depend on the selection of sources			
7	I can explain how and why different historical interpretations have been produced. I can show how attitudes and circumstances can influence an individual's interpretation of historical events or developments. I can explain why different groups or societies interpret history in different ways			
8	I can analyse and explain different historical interpretations and am beginning to evaluate them			

	Historical enquiry			
2	I can answer questions about the past, from sources of information, on the basis of simple observations			
3	I can make deductions from historical sources			
4	I can put together information drawn from different historical sources			
5	Using my historical knowledge and understanding, I am beginning to evaluate sources of information and identify those that are useful for particular tasks			
6	Using my historical knowledge and understanding, I can identify and evaluate sources of information which I use critically to reach and support conclusions. I can show how a source which is unreliable can nevertheless be useful			
7	I am beginning to show independence in following lines of enquiry, using my knowledge and understanding to identify, evaluate and use sources of information critically by referring to the circumstances in which they were produced. I show an understanding that a source can be more or less valuable depending on the questions asked of it			
8	Drawing on my historical knowledge and understanding, I use sources of information critically. I carry out enquiries about historical topics, and independently reach substantiated conclusions			
	Organisation and communication			
2	I can demonstrate factual knowledge and understanding of aspects of the past beyond living memory and of some of the main events and people I have studied			
3	I can demonstrate factual knowledge and understanding of some of the main events, people and changes drawn from the study units			
4	I am starting to produce structured work, making appropriate use of dates and terms			
5	I select and organise relevant information to produce structured work, making appropriate use of dates and terms			
6	I select, organise and deploy relevant information to produce structured work, making appropriate use of dates and terms			

7	I am beginning to reach substantiated conclusions independently. I can select, organise and deploy relevant information to produce well-structured narratives and descriptions, making appropriate use of dates and terms			
8	I select, organise and deploy relevant information to produce consistently well-structured narratives, descriptions and explanations, making appropriate use of dates and terms			
	GCSE Sourcework Skills *[The following are to be achieved at Grade C level before being ticked]*			
2	I understand how to make inferences from sources			
3	I can assess the extent to which a source provides sufficient information on a topic			
4	I can assess the reliability of a source to a topic			
5	I can assess the usefulness of a source to a topic			
6	I can explain why two interpretations of the same events differ			
7	I can assess the reliability of two interpretations			

Why study history?

Finally, if anyone asks 'Why study history?', try this poem:

No Mystery

Do you know what is meant by a wooden horse?
Do you know that Italians ruled Britain by force?
Imagine a king who beheaded his wives
And a Great War, so great it cost millions of lives.

A little Napoleon – what does that mean?
The Diet of Worms – imagine the scene!
Why was it built, that canal near your home?
And why's it an issue – the right to roam?

Does Magna Carta mean nothing to you?
Did she die in vain? (Or isn't that true?)
Why did Martin Luther King have a dream?
And why does Croatia have its own football team?

Did you hear that Britannia once ruled the waves?
But the Empire strikes back, and so did the slaves.
Americans tipped British tea in the water.
My Lai, Wounded Knee, Dresden, Dachau – all slaughter.

The news of today gets old pretty fast
The present and future turn into the past.
So what is the secret? It's no mystery.
It's where we all come from. It's history!

Notes